Sales Promotion Decision Making

Sales Promotion Decision Making

Concepts, Principles, and Practice

Steve Ogden-Barnes and Stella Minahan

First published in 2015 by
Business Expert Press, LLC
222 East 46th Street, New York, NY 10017
www.businessexpertpress.com

ISBN-13: 978-1-63157-047-6 (paperback)
ISBN-13: 978-1-63157-048-3 (e-book)

Business Expert Press Marketing Strategy Collection

Collection ISSN: 2150-9654 (print)
Collection ISSN: 2150-9662 (electronic)

Cover and interior design by Exeter Premedia Services Private Ltd.,
Chennai, India

First edition: 2015

10 9 8 7 6 5 4 3 2 1

Printed in the United States of America.

Abstract

Sales promotions are a *fact of life* for the majority of retailers, suppliers, and FMGC stakeholders commanding up to 75 percent of total marketing budgets. From straightforward discounts on products to more complex omni-channel consumer competitions and contests, sales promotions play a vital role as both strategic and tactical marketing tools. Those responsible for sales promotions must deliver real results in cut-throat competitive trading environments. However, with limited understanding of the options, principles, and practices that underpin effective sales promotion planning, managers often rely on past experience or preferences to guide their decision making. Not surprisingly, many sales promotions fail to achieve their potential. This book serves as a vital resource for practitioners. Distilled from over 700 articles and cases, it presents the findings of comprehensive global research which explores the DNA of sales promotions including their role, nature, and function, the critical decision-making processes and campaign evaluation. This is supported with case studies of sales promotion planning in practice based on research conducted in FMCG and retail organizations. The book offers the reader a deeper, more comprehensive, and critical expert appreciation of the core concepts that define sales promotions. This will empower decision makers, consultants, and stakeholders to make more confident, informed, and effective campaign decisions.

Keywords

advertising, consumer promotions, decision making, marketing, monetary promotions, nonmonetary promotions, retail, sales promotion

Contents

CHAPTER 1

Sales Promotions and the New World of Retail

Introduction

This chapter serves two main purposes: it introduces the reader to sales promotions as a distinct and vital topic within marketing and it highlights the significance of effective sales promotions management in a dynamic, competitive environment, where effective decision making is more important than ever. The chapter also summarizes the key aims of the book and the rationale for its timely publication. We argue managers with responsibility for sales promotion management require a deeper understanding of the nature and efficacy of the alternatives available to them to optimize their significant investment in campaigns and initiatives.

Overview of the Book

Buy one get one free, below cost price, 20 percent off, clearance sale, new improved product, the best available, 25 words or less, redeem coupons, and *online competition* are all examples of sales promotions available to the marketer and the retailer. Sales promotions—what they are, how they can be used, and the decision-making process—are the focus of this book. Specifically, we look at the role of sales promotions within the general marketing framework. We argue that given the pervasiveness, associated costs and brand impact of sales promotions are worthy of sustained and critical attention.

To begin, we describe some of the challenges faced by the retail industry with an emphasis on how consumers' purchasing habits and buying power have changed. These changes in consumer behavior have led to new demands across the supply chain. In order to remain viable, retailers must be constantly evolving their skills to meet the demands and challenges of this new retail environment.

We explore the challenges facing retailers around the globe. In an age of modern global consumerism, many retail sectors have seen an explosion of market entrants occupying a variety of competitive positions: mass, niche, value, discount, and convenience, for example. In addition, the industry has faced an exponential rise in the popularity of Internet shopping.

Would that Promotion Work Here?

Literature in the field of sales promotions is often hard to find and sometimes contradictory. For example, many academics and practitioners focus exclusively on price discounting tactics, while others present generic and sometimes overly complex models and frameworks that purport to show how decisions should be made. Invariably, these approaches are criticized because they are not relevant or effective in real-world scenarios where operational dynamics, the experience of decision makers, company sector and culture, and internal and external influences all merge to create a unique decision-making environment not readily navigated with *off the shelf* tools. Guidance often takes the form of a series of checklist questions, without presenting the rationale behind these questions. Sometimes marketing magazines and agencies present glossy overviews of sales promotion campaigns that have yielded positive results, but without the critical insight or comprehensive understanding of the reasons why specific campaign factors were chosen. This lack of knowledge and insight makes it difficult for practitioners to assess the potential of a particular campaign for their own organization.

The authors of this book all have longstanding industry and research profiles in the field of marketing, retailing, advertising, and sales promotion. We are conscious of the fact that although there is a vast body of academic and practitioner information relating to sales promotions, it is often difficult for the busy professional to access and digest succinct sources that have mainstream practical relevance. Many books could be written about each of the myriad of interrelated sales promotion tactics: discounting, pricing, merchandising, and coupons to name but a few. However, the authors believe that there was a need for a book that gets a business professional up to speed with the topic overall, without compromising readability or accessibility. This will provide the confidence and inspiration to delve more deeply into further areas of interest.

Scope of the Research

The research presented in this book is the result of five years of primary and secondary research. The authors interviewed marketing decision makers in diverse consumer-focused organizations. Over 700 academic papers, business cases, and articles were reviewed, critiqued, and analyzed to distil the key messages and learnings.

The research revealed that managers often have limited understanding of the concepts and principles that underpin sales promotions and rely on past experience or preferences to guide their decision making. We argue that the scale of the sales promotion budget calls for a more disciplined and informed management approach.

Aims of the Book

The authors believe that in order to make more effective sales promotion decisions, managers need to have a robust, in-depth working knowledge of the world of sales promotions presented in an accessible form. The key aims of the book are:

- To educate and inform about the intrinsic nature of diverse forms of sales promotions, including their role, rationale, nature and function, key decision-making processes, and campaign evaluation methods in a concise, user-friendly form.
- To inform the time-poor reader about the *how* and *why* of sales promotion effectiveness, focusing on the function, benefits, advantages, and limitations of diverse promotional options.
- To share research that has been conducted into consumers' perceptions and reactions to help the reader understand the factors that influence consumers' response and engagement.
- To illustrate the realities of sales promotion practice by sharing the results of original research conducted with

decision makers in a sample of retail and consumer-facing businesses: retailers, manufacturers, buying groups, suppliers, and campaign agencies.

- To demystify the complex world of sales promotions with clear definitions and succinct overviews of the pros and cons of campaign alternatives to provide a common platform for discussion and debate, and highlight where further, more in-depth research, knowledge, and advice may be needed.

This book, while using concepts and models to structure discussion, does not do so in a prescriptive way. Rather, it aims to provide the reader with a sufficient body of knowledge to facilitate more critical, objective, and effective decision making in relation to the campaigns they manage.

The authors of this book are strong advocates of an evidence-driven approach to decision making, capitalizing on the extensive body of knowledge that exists to inform and guide decisions. Rigid frameworks and generic models have their acknowledged limitations. Using and interpreting research to shape thinking and define culturally relevant decision approaches increases both the quality of decisions and the effectiveness of outcomes. This book is our way of supporting an evidence-based approach to decision making in the dynamic field of sales promotion.

This book has value for the early career and seasoned professionals from marketing, advertising, purchasing, and category management as well as sales promotion planners and agency consultants. The insights are particularly relevant for retailers and their manufacturers and suppliers due to the increasing popularity of promotions in a challenging—and evolving—trading environment.

Dynamic World of Retail

There has been a fundamental change in how we shop. Internet-savvy consumers now compare features, prices, offers, and online deals before purchasing. Globally, mobile technologies and smartphones have added a new dimension to the omni-channel retail world, placing real-time price and product visibility firmly in the hands of the bricks and mortar shopper. For example, many consumers now participate in the activity known as *showrooming*. This is when shoppers inspect products in a physical store, then compare competitor pricing and availability via mobile devices, sometimes purchasing from another source while in a store. In response, some retailers have experimented with charging shoppers who view in-store but do not purchase (Knight 2013). This issue is significant with one survey showing that 36 percent of consumers engaged in showrooming (Jude and Singh 2012). For some retailers, the combined challenges of this rapid retail evolution have simply been too great, with some long-established brands disappearing from the sector forever. The consumer now researches and shops differently. This is a new retail paradigm as the balance of power has shifted toward the consumer. The retail industry must be more responsive, more informed, and more skillful in order to meet these challenges.

Retail: A Game of Skill

Retail is an industry that demands world-class operational competence in many areas. Knowledge and skills are required in information technology, buying, merchandise management, marketing and promotion, distribution, human resources, and consumer service. In order to be profitable and successful in these challenging times, retailers and suppliers must be at the top of their game across all of these areas, mastering strategy and optimizing capital investments. Effective decision making in these areas is vital for moving the product through the supply chain profitably to the point of purchase. In this book, we focus on strategies and tactics that underpin effective decision making in sales promotion in particular. Sales promotions provide the motivation for consumers to purchase products at the final stage of a product supply chain journey, resulting in the sales transaction, which is the life blood of the retail industry.

Sales Promotions in Focus

Sales promotions are vital strategic and tactical tools within the marketing value chain. In their various forms, they perform multiple roles and meet diverse objectives. Research has continued to illustrate the significance of sales promotions as a core marketing activity (Gardener and Trivedi

1998; Haskins and Hugli 1969; Jobber 1973; Kimball 1989; Peattie, Peattie, and Emafo 1997; Ziliani 2006). Furthermore, there has been a significant increase in the marketing budgets allocated to sales promotions. Estimates of the proportions of marketing budgets allocated to sales promotions vary considerably but range between 25 and 75 percent of total marketing spend (Palazon and Delgado-Ballester 2009; Spears 2010). It is essential therefore to ensure that an optimal return on the promotional spend is achieved.

They can be the catalyst to encourage:

- Store or website visitation
- Profitable changes in consumer behavior
- Purchase of greater volumes of products
- Shoppers to buy new products
- Trial of different brands

They can be used to launch new lines or to clear old stock. They can also act as a mechanism for collecting vital consumer information and serve as a tactical response to counter aggressive competitor activity.

Challenges for the Professional

There are many professional staff employed by manufacturers, agents, retailers, and advertisers who are responsible for sales promotion planning and implementation. Their role is to establish objectives, evaluate options, and negotiate outcomes to ensure that their initiatives deliver real results. They have to do this in dynamic, culturally diverse decision-making environments filled with a variety of sometimes conflicting opinions. This book is addressed to these practitioners.

Managers make decisions all the time in their professional capacities. Many decisions are straightforward or routine, while others will be more complex, critical, and significant. Managers do no always stop to consider and reflect upon their decision-making processes. Instead, they use a mix of insight, hindsight, experience, data, and negotiation to reach a solution. And they will always be judged on the effectiveness of their decisions by the results. Organizational culture and peer influence play a strong role and this is especially true in marketing decision making where there is seldom a *black or white* choice available, with evaluation sometimes being complex and contentious. This is understandable considering the time and task pressures that managers face.

Not surprisingly, many sales promotions fail to achieve their full potential with some analysts estimating as few as 17 percent achieve profitability targets (Kotler 2009). Consequently, there has been long-running and strong criticism leveled at those responsible for the perceived ad hoc and sometimes maverick approach to planning and decision making. This criticism also extends to marketing and advertising more generally, but sales promotions—with their high investment costs, high visibility, time-limited offer, and critical strategic and tactical significance—have arguably been most prominent in the firing line.

We also note that there is little opportunity for professionals to learn about successful sales promotion management. Imagine, for example, a young graduate embarking on a marketing career. Their entry to the world of sales promotions can be fraught with confusion and complexity as they navigate ingrained preferences, assertive campaign partners, creative agency pitches, powerful stakeholders, and the all-important budgeting discussions and campaign evaluation exercises. Sales promotions are studied at colleges and universities, but seldom in any great detail compared to the emphasis placed on marketing, advertising, and consumer behavior.

Chapter Highlights

- Retail is now a globalized, omni-channel industry.
- Effective decision making is more essential than ever.
- Sales promotions are vital to shopper engagement.
- It is important to understand the complexity, variety, and application of promotional alternatives.
- Many decision makers do not appreciate the nuances of options available.
- As result of these dynamics, sales promotions often fail to achieve their full potential.

CHAPTER 2

The Many Faces of Sales Promotions

Consumers face a variety of sales promotions designed to influence their choices of products. Coupons, rebates, bonus sizes, "buy one, get one" offers, sweepstakes, and product premiums, gifts with purchase are all promotional tools directed toward consumers that allow firms to achieve short-term results such as increased market share or unit sales. What these promotions have in common is provision of some extra utility to the consumer, primarily through direct monetary savings. (Fogel and Thornton 2008, 31)

Introduction

This chapter sets the scene for the research presented later in the book in which specific categories of sales promotion are discussed. It contextualizes sales promotions within the marketing and advertising decision-making fields. It summarizes some of the major debates that define the sales promotion research agenda and distinguishes the two main forms of sales promotion: monetary and nonmonetary. The chapter also highlights the major considerations for campaign planners relating to customer engagement and the timing of reward or benefit realization.

Sales Promotions in Context

Sales promotions and the decisions made by managers that relate to them cannot be viewed in isolation. They must be seen as part of a wider agenda that extends to the fields of marketing and advertising. Promotions are, after all, developed to support the wider competitive business aims encapsulated in the *marketing plan*. They will also share the stage (and sometimes compete for funding) with advertising strategies and initiatives. A concise understanding of the marketing and advertising decision-making arenas is essential to enable sales promotions to be viewed in context.

Marketing Planning

The complex and challenging landscape outlined in Chapter 1 demands that businesses create and communicate a unique position in over-crowded markets. Clearly a well-defined and robust marketing strategy is central to this aim, with a detailed marketing planning operationalizing the specifics of the familiar *4Ps*: product, place, price, and promotion. Marketing planning is defined as "the development of marketing strategy, and design and implementation of marketing programs" (Dibb 2002, 442).

The marketing plan is the formal document that defines and communicates the decisions made within the marketing planning process.

Marketing in the Spotlight

The diversity and efficacy of marketing decision-making approaches have been widely explored and debated in recent years. As marketing evolves to encompass new channels and technologies, the *art versus science* debate has intensified, with some advocating a data-driven intelligence and insight-based approach, while others champion the value of entrepreneurship, experience, and gut feel. There is continuing debate between theorists and marketing practitioners as to what constitutes best practice decision-making approaches. One writer summarized the heart of this debate identifying that there was:

> Little clarity and hence confusion among theorists and prac-titioners … Managers are likely to choose ideas, models and techniques which they understand, find easy to use, and which resonate in their business context. Whether this chosen "technol-ogy" is also the best or most appropriate is, of course, an entirely different matter. (Franklin 2001, 344)

Further, criticism has been leveled at the lack of rigor in practical marketing decision making, and there are calls for professional bodies to do more to develop standards (Corkindale 2009, 19). In this case, the author claimed that "some marketers probably only know about half of what they should about the concepts they use."

Marketing Measures

Perhaps due to these polarized views, marketing as a business function continues to receive its fair share of criticism, especially in relation to its ability to prove its worth through its return on investment. This creates the potential for tension and conflict based on "uncertainty about the return on marketing dollars" (Marshall 2007, 46). Furthermore, and perhaps compounded by this, it has been proposed that the marketing function may suffer from what could be viewed as *image issues* within an organization, based on perceptions of poor control of spending and a loose evaluation of marketing investment impact (See 2006). Proving marketing's worth remains a persistent challenge for practitioners, largely due to the fact that identifying the parameters of its influence both long and short term and defining comprehensive measures of effectiveness is problematic.

The question of evaluation and return on investment is an especially contentious issue in the debate on marketing impact. There is a case to be made for an objective measure of the impact of strategic marketing decisions, especially as accountability has been identified as a key factor in defining the degree of influence a marketing department exercises within the business (Verhoef and Leeflang 2009), with more effective marketing evaluation raising trust levels (Solcansky and Simberova 2010). But just how can the impact of something so far reaching and sometimes as intangible as marketing be objectively evaluated? Some researchers have advocated that the basic evaluation criteria of, for example, sales growth, is no longer effective in calculating either true cost or real benefit, and a more holistic and scientific measurement is required. Others have encouraged a focus on return on marketing investment (ROMI) measurement and have criticized the industry for not doing enough in relation to this

(Cook and Talluri 2004). ROMI as a tool of decision evaluation and performance management has received both academic and industry attention, with commentators seeking to promote the process and benefits as well as dispel criticisms of ROMI as a key measure (Gow 2007; Lenskold 2007). Although there is a commonly expressed view that it is essential to evaluate marketing activities, there is a noted lack of consensus on exactly how this evaluation should be managed. The debate on the measurement of marketing effectiveness has a long history and diverse viewpoints, with alternative measures, for example, ROTPI (return on touch point investment) (Schultz, Cole, and Bailey 2004), EAV (expected advertising value) (Ducoffe and Curlo 2000), and the valuation of intangible assets (including goodwill) (Olsen and Halliwell 2007) also being advocated.

Lively discussion therefore continues between those who champion theory, models, and a scientific approach to decision making and those who place greater emphasis on understanding the contribution of intuition and judgment. In what is a dynamic, intuitive decision-making context, these themes are also echoed in the advertising realm.

Advertising and Sales Promotion: Related, but Different

It is important to clearly distinguish between advertising and promotion. Advertising in its broadest sense has been defined as "an indirect way of turning a potential customer towards the advertised product or service by providing information that is designed to effect a favourable impression" (Percy and Elliott 2005, 4).

This highlights the Latin origins of the word as *to turn toward*, positioning advertising as a means by which to direct a consumer toward a brand or product. Sales promotions are portrayed as a means by which to capitalize upon this attention—a call to action for the consumer.

Advertising in Focus

"Little is known about the day-to-day struggles of managers who are faced with setting and allocating these (advertising) budgets" (Low and Mohr 1999, 67).

Experts have—as with marketing decision making—proposed models and frameworks in an attempt to guide more objective and effective advertising decision making. It is possible that the call for greater objectivity and the use of models in advertising decision making is falling on deaf ears, taking into account the professional mindset and industry culture. Research into how managers in the United States and Western Europe make advertising budget and allocation decisions revealed a distinctly intuitive approach (Permut 1977). Some advertising professionals were observed to operate with "vague descriptions of advertising objectives, arbitrary budget and media decisions and lack of control with the advertising results" (Helgesen 1992, 30).

A significant criticism of advertising decision-making models is that they all too often focus on the direct relationship between advertising spend and sales revenues over a fixed period of time, but do not consider the long-term effects of advertising that may transcend the measurement period (Picconi and Olson 1978). As with marketing, the comprehensive evaluation of impact and contribution remains challenging. Advertising management practices is therefore a contentious area, perhaps due to the perceived difficulties in identifying what works and what does not and calculating the tangible return on advertising dollars spent. One writer concluded: "we may not now, or ever, know definitively how advertising works" (Vaughn 1986, 65).

Despite the criticisms of decision-making approaches, it is also important to remember that advertising is in essence a creative process, with one academic lamenting the lack of appreciation for this from those who judge the work of creative teams (Mondroski, Reid, and Russell 1983). As with marketing decision making, there is evidence of a divide between theory and practice in this field. Gaining consensus on optimal decision-making approaches may therefore remain elusive. Sales promotion professionals—by association—may often fall under the same, cool gaze as those who hold responsibility for marketing or advertising strategies. Although they are distinct professional disciplines, it is important to acknowledge their interrelatedness and their interdependence. It is also vital to acknowledge the commonalities in terms of management approach, decision methods, and evaluation that define critical debate.

Sales Promotions Under Fire

The term *sales promotion* refers to a wide variety of campaigns and initiatives all designed to encourage consumers to buy, buy more, or buy more often. Considering and comparing these choices in their promotional planning activities, decision makers must also consider how effective a specific method will be in achieving these particular aims and objectives.

Research Landscape

Due to the scale and scope of corporate spending on sales promotions, there has been significant research conducted into sales promotions management. Some commentators have offered specific criticism of the lack of organizational control over promotional spending, and have questioned, for example, "why is so much money being spent on promotions, and why is this spending increasing with so little pressure from executive management to control it?" (Struse 1987, 151). Others challenge the long-term negative impact on brand equity and sales that some forms of sales promotions may have (Ataman, van Heerde, and Mela 2010; Simonson, Carmon, and O'Curry 1994), reflective of a view of sales promotion that they can cheapen the brand and cannibalize future business. Furthermore, concerns have been raised about the apparent disparity between textbook approaches and practices on the ground.

Extensive research has been conducted into price-based (monetary) promotions, with specific reference to what the impact of varying degrees of price promotions is on consumer perception, buying behavior, profitability, and performance (Ehrenberg, Hammond, and Goodhardt 1994; Gardner and Strang 1984; Jedidi, Mela, and Gupta 1999; Simester 1997; Srinivasan et al. 2004; van Heerde 2005). This research has often utilized staple consumer goods as the product focus (Ailawadi and Neslin 1998; Peterson 1969; Rajagopal 2008; Sun, Neslin, and Srinivasan 2003), due to the high volumes of sales and the relative ease of accessing point-of-sale (POS) data. The influences and effects of nonmonetary, or *value-adding* sales promotions are considered to be less well explored (Shu-Ling 2006) but are now receiving more research attention (Palazón-Vidal and Delgado-Ballester 2009). There have also been concerns expressed relating to the methods managers use to decide on promotional strategies.

Research conducted into management approaches has revealed a reliance on past strategies and an undisciplined approach to evaluation. This supports a picture of managers who may in reality implement a large number of sales promotions hoping that at least some will be successful (Simpson 2006).

Choice and Decisions

Each promotional alternative offers potential advantages and disadvantages to the organization, category, product, or customer, but all present decision makers with challenges relating to choice, design, implementation, and evaluation. Some campaign options are considered more suitable than others in serving specific goals, and therefore skill and insight are required to ensure that the best campaign option is chosen. In defining their promotional strategies, managers must address the following key questions:

1. *What are my choices?*
2. *What are we rewarding?*
3. *At what point should the promotional benefit be realized by the consumer?*
4. *Is the promotion right for the target consumer?*
5. *Should we collaborate with suppliers or partners?*

It is important to explore the implications of these top-line questions before focusing on specific campaign alternatives. This will ensure that promotional strategies will be built on firm foundations and that a clear understanding of the context of campaign decision making is in place.

What Are My Choices?

Sales promotions are presented to consumers by retailers, manufacturers, agents, suppliers, or distributors on a daily basis. Regardless of ownership, sales promotions fall into one of two camps: monetary or nonmonetary.

> **Monetary promotions:** These offer consumers an incentive to purchase by amending the price of an item. They offer a tangible financial incentive to the consumer, often in the form of a discount.

Nonmonetary promotions: These provide consumers with an incentive to purchase by offering additional value, without necessarily changing price.

A Question of Definition

The definitions of these major forms of promotion vary in literature. Overall, *monetary promotions* are often associated with discounting. *Nonmonetary promotions* take many forms and are sometimes referred to as *premium promotions*.

The most common options within each of these categories are summarized in Table 2.1.

These will be explored in more detail in later chapters, but as can be seen, there is a wide range of campaign choices for the manager to consider. In complex competitive environments—where multiple promotions run simultaneously—defining the mix, messaging, and timing of these promotions is a complex task requiring advanced planning, co-ordination, and control skills.

What Are We Rewarding?

For promotional planners, it is important to consider exactly what behavior or actions are being targeted to ensure that the campaign design elicits the desired response. Does the campaign align to these intentions by encouraging the desired behavior? In one interview conducted for this book, there was an example of a campaign that although intended to increase the average spend per visit offered a reward in the form of a

Table 2.1 Major forms of sales promotions

Monetary promotions	Nonmonetary promotions
Discounting:	Bonus pack size
Dollar off price discount	Buy one get one free (BOGOF)
Cent off price discount	Free gift with purchase
Percentage off discount	Product bundling
Was/is discount	Sampling
Couponing	Embedded premiums
Rebates	Competitions, sweepstakes, and contests

sweepstake entry for spending at the current average spend threshold. This promotion therefore rewarded current purchase behavior and would have been unlikely to change purchase habits in support of the stated objective.

At What Point Should the Promotional Benefit Be Realized by the Consumer?

Whether monetary or nonmonetary, a key consideration facing promotional planners and designers is the question of when the promotional benefits should be realized by the consumer. For some promotions, the benefit is immediate, while in other cases the benefit is delayed, perhaps subject to a future action by the consumer. To explain this we can refer to *front-loaded* or *rear-loaded* promotions. In simple terms, a discount is considered to provide the shopper with an immediate benefit (front-loaded), while the offer of discount on a future purchase or a rebate provides a delayed benefit and is therefore a rear-loaded incentive (Zhang, Krishna, and Dhar 2000). Research in this field (Kim 2013) proposes that factors including whether the purchase type is likely to initiate either risk or variety seeking purchase behavior (i.e., confectionary), or risk-resistant choice (i.e., strong brand categories like detergent) should prompt consideration of the timing of reward activation. It concluded that for a risk-seeking shopper, a delayed reward is probably preferable: These shoppers may be happy to take a chance regardless of any immediate incentive. The research in this case confirmed the view that for products and categories that attract a variety-seeking mindset, rear-loaded promotions are the most effective, with the opposite being true for risk-resistant consumers where an *upfront* incentive to purchase will have more influence.

Is the Promotion Right for the Target Consumer?

Offering promotions is one thing, but it is important to consider the degree to which consumers look favorably upon, and are likely to respond to the deal. Some shoppers will be highly price and value conscious and receptive to offers put in front of them, manifesting what is termed *deal proneness* (Rao 2009). Others may be less *deal prone* and therefore less inclined to capitalize on the offers presented. Knowing what proportion of your customer base is deal prone, or which products and categories attract promotion-hungry shoppers, can help to effectively target promotional spending.

Many people prefer a simple life and this philosophy also extends to our lives as shoppers. A lot of time and effort goes into presenting creative and compelling sales promotions, but this good work can go to waste if consumers perceive that securing the benefits is just too much trouble, or a *hassle*—as these authors explain:

> We suggest that some types of promotions impose more hassles on consumers than others. These hassles can be due to increased cognitive load, physical handling, or both. Examples of hassles associated with cognitive effort include remembering to use a coupon before it expires, making sure the correct brand-size unit is chosen, remembering to use a peel-off coupon at the register, and keeping track of whether one has fulfilled the requirements associated with various contests, rebates, or gifts with purchase. (Fogel and Thornton 2008, 34)

If the aim of a promotion is to maximize consumption and provide utilitarian benefits, then campaign designers need to consider the degree of *hassle* involved in understanding, interpreting, and responding to the campaign. A larger benefit may encourage more effort on the part of the shopper and some promotions that appeal to more hedonic motivations may be deliberately complex and challenging. It is important to remember that in most cases the aim is to get the product in the shopping basket, not the *too hard* basket.

Should We Collaborate with Suppliers or Partners?

Promotions can be managed independently by a business, or in partnership with suppliers and partners. Rather than be seen as an activity owned by and benefiting either the manufacturer or the vendor, there is a strong case for collaborative promotions whereby the costs of a discount, for example, are shared by both parties in proportion to their original margins. This is one way to optimize the profitability of discounting (argued to be largely suboptimal) for both parties across chosen channels (Wierenga and Soethoudt 2010). By more accurate modeling and forecasting and with closer collaboration between retailer and supplier, it has been proposed that up to a 31 percent increase in promotional effectiveness is achievable (Kopalle, Mela, and Marsh 1999). If promotional dips (especially pre-promotion) are evident, it is a tell-tale sign that shoppers may be wise to promotional tactics and are taking full and strategic advantage of discounting initiatives.

Deal-Maker ... or Breaker

Sales promotions present those responsible for their planning and execution with a wide range of options and alternatives. As identified, managers may not always fully consider the implications of their choices, relying instead on intuition and experience. They may also not focus enough on the fine detail in planning and execution that could make the difference between a successful campaign and a poor one. Central to sales promotion success for any business is choosing objectively the most appropriate campaign mechanism for the business, brand, category, or product objectives which are specified. The next two chapters focus on defining and exploring the diversity of monetary and nonmonetary promotion available to decision makers.

Chapter Highlights

- It is important to distinguish marketing advertising and sales promotions.
- These three interrelated disciplines share common ground in terms in the critical management agenda.
- The term *sales promotion* encompasses a wide range of campaigns and initiatives.
- Sales promotion decision-making practices are often criticized for a lack of control and an undisciplined approach.

- There is a noted theory–practice divide in the field.
- The major forms of sales promotions are monetary and nonmonetary.
- Managers must address key questions of choice, design, timing, reward, and benefit.
- Sales promotions may be run with or without supplier or partner involvement.

CHAPTER 3

Roles, Functions, and Benefits

Introduction

This chapter addresses the central question of why sales promotions are so popular and prevalent. It looks at the roles, functions, and benefits available to key stakeholder groups including retailers, suppliers and manufacturers, and consumers. The use of sales promotions by service industries and the not-for-profit sectors is discussed. We consider why promotional investment has increased in scale (Blattberg, Briesch, and Fox 1995) and grown in relation to *above the line* activities, including mainstream advertising (Hartley and Cross 1988). An understanding of these matters is argued to be central to effective decision making.

Sales Promotion: Roles, Functions, and Benefits

For businesses in competitive markets, sales promotions are highly flexible marketing tools. They are commonly used by retailers, manufacturers, and suppliers. The use of sales promotions has also been researched in relation to charitable and not-for-profit organizations (Marcotte 1989; Peattie 2003), service providers (Peattie and Peattie 1995), and the government (Cowell 1984; Quelch and Jocz 2010). They serve many purposes and offer numerous advantages including the following:

1. Correcting or increasing sales performance
2. Attracting new shoppers
3. Increasing average spend per visit
4. Increasing purchase quantity
5. Increasing cross-category sales
6. Seasonal demand smoothing
7. Launching a new product or category

8. Brand building/rewarding loyalty
9. Tactical competitor response
10. Employee engagement

Correcting or Increasing Sales Performance

Sales promotions can provide a short-term boost to sales at key times of the year, or when it appears sales forecasts for particular products or categories may not be achieved. Providing an extra incentive to shoppers to make a purchase they might otherwise not have completed can transcend mainstream advertising and make the difference between a consumer purchasing or merely browsing. These additional sales can help to bring sales performance back on track.

Attracting New Shoppers

Creative and captivating sales promotions can be used with advertising to increase market share by attracting new consumers at the expense of the competition.

Increasing Average Spend Per Visit

Retailers can motivate consumers to spend more per visit by offering them promotional incentives. This can increase the average transaction size. Retailers can, for example, offer a promotion that rewards shoppers for spending more than the average basket value.

Increasing Purchase Quantity

Sales promotions that reward consumers for buying more SKUs (stock keeping units) or larger pack sizes of products can help retailers increase the quantity or volume of products sold. From the consumer's perspective, this may mean *stockpiling* products. If the rate of consumption of the product does not increase, household stocks will last longer, therefore impacting future purchase rates. This type of promotion can therefore have a detrimental effect on future sales.

Increasing Cross-Category Sales

Sales promotions can encourage cross-category selling. For example, a promotion may offer an incentive to a consumer to buy pasta and a related kitchen product, such as utensils or olive oil.

Seasonal Demand Smoothing

Highs and lows in product demand can create a major problem for retailers and their suppliers as they try to effectively manage inventory levels, production, and supply. For products that are prone to strong demand peaks over a season, sales promotions can be used to stimulate demand, encouraging consumers to purchase more of the product at times when demand usually declines.

Launching a New Product or Category

To draw attention to a new line or department, many retailers (or suppliers) will combine a new launch with a promotion. As the product is new, this is unlikely to be a price discount, but may include a free gift with purchase, or an in-store demonstration or a promotional competition. Consumers sometimes need an extra incentive to change their entrenched purchase behaviors or brand preferences. A targeted sale promotion can provide the extra push required for shoppers to try something new.

Brand Building and Rewarding Loyalty

Well-designed sales promotions—especially ones that are not discount-based—can be a great way to keep consumers engaged with a brand. The promotion may be linked to loyalty programs. For example, high-spend shoppers may be invited to participate in an exclusive, *invitation only* event such as a fashion evening. Even during a quiet time of year for consumer communications, sales promotion can keep the dialogue—and the transactions—flowing.

Tactical Competitor Response

Businesses keep their marketing and promotional plans close to their chest, and as a consequence competitor activity can sometimes catch the business off guard. This can be when an aggressive price-promise campaign is launched or an exclusive range is announced. Sales promotions present the retailer with the option to launch a rapid, tactical counter-offensive.

Employee Engagement

A great promotion, well planned and well executed, can serve to create a real in-store buzz with employees. New products, vibrant point of sale, and invigorated shoppers will serve to lift the atmosphere and energy in-store. This is providing that store management and staff understand the rationale for the event and the logistics of in-store execution have been well considered and communicated in a timely fashion.

Suppliers and Manufacturers

Suppliers and manufacturers gain benefits and advantages from participating in sales promotions. These benefits include the following:

1. Negotiating advantage
2. New brand or product profile raising
3. Encouraging brand switching and growing market share
4. Motivating or rewarding sales associates
5. Proactive response to category sales target achievement
6. Preserving margins and brand integrity

Negotiating Advantage

Suppliers and manufacturers often compete for business and for shelf space. In essence, it is easier for vendors to source an alternative supplier than it is for a supplier to source an alternative outlet for their products. As part of the on-going negotiation process, businesses will often expect their suppliers to develop a synergistic marketing and promotional plan, detailing how the proposed product or range will be supported over the course of its product lifecycle. Hence, sales promotions increasingly form part of a supplier's negotiating strategy along with more mainstream activities including consumer research, advertising, and sponsorship. In supplier markets where products may be easy to substitute, this can be strong value-adding for retail consumers.

New Brand or Product Profile Raising

As new products are launched to the market or developed and upgraded, trade promotions that communicate innovative features and benefits can be used to create awareness and interest among potential or existing users.

Encouraging Brand Switching and Growing Market Share

Special deals or incentives can encourage consumers to switch brands temporarily—or permanently. For *challenger* brands, this is perhaps more critical as they seek to take market share from more established players and need to motivate consumers to change their purchase behavior.

Motivating or Rewarding Sales Associates

Rather than leaving product sales to chance, some suppliers run trade promotions that encourage consumer-facing staff to take a more active role in promoting their products to undecided consumers. This may be solely directed at sales staff, or may be run in parallel with a consumer-focused promotion to maximize impact.

Proactive Response to Category Sales Target Achievement

Manufacturers and suppliers are naturally keen to ensure that the sales targets agreed in buyer negotiations are achieved and exceeded. This reduces the risk of a reduction in space allocation, maintains the return on investment of any levies or charges made, and may ultimately prevent or at least delay delisting. Maintaining a proactive and collaborative stance on sales performance management will ensure that the need for promotional activity can be anticipated and planned well in advance, using historic sales data and forecasting.

Preserving Margins and Brand Integrity

When faced with the prospect of markdowns due to poor sales, suppliers may prefer to negotiate a promotion as an alternative to losing margins through discounting. This approach may also preserve brand integrity as the products are not overly associated with price-based promotions that may cheapen the brand.

It is clear that the benefits of sales promotions are available to the suppliers and manufacturers as well as to retailers. Most importantly, it is the consumers who must perceive the value of the sales promotions and be willing participants in the sales promotions.

Consumers

For consumers, sales promotions can offer a variety of benefits including better prices and savings, better value, novel brand engagement experiences, enjoyment, education, stimulation, and retail theatre. Without their willing and enthusiastic engagement, sales promotions would fail. For the industry as a whole, it is important that sales promotions are not over used, which can result in *promotion fatigue*. Evidence suggests that promotions overall are becoming less effective because of their prevalence:

> In 70 percent of package-goods categories last year, at least 30 percent of merchandise was sold with some kind of promotional support ... that's up from 60 percent of categories four years ago. In all, two-thirds of categories saw increased promotional support last year. But average volume lift per merchandising event declined across more than half (57 percent) of CPG categories last year. "We do believe there's a level of promotion fatigue out there." (Neff 2011)

This implies that consumers may simply be so over-exposed to deals, offers, and specials that their impact diminishes. It is not just in the retail sector that promotions are used to influence purchase behavior.

Having now defined what sales promotions are and explored their role and benefits they offer, the following chapters provide a more detailed understanding of the major forms of specific sales promotions, both monetary and nonmonetary.

Chapter Highlights

- Sales promotions perform a variety of value-adding roles and functions.
- They can offer significant potential benefits.
- The key stakeholders in sales promotion management are retailers, suppliers, manufacturers, and consumers.
- Sales promotions have not-for-profit applications.
- Businesses need to be aware of the potential for *promotion fatigue*.

CHAPTER 4

Monetary Promotions

Introduction

In this chapter, we explore the world of monetary promotions. In their attempts to attract consumers, many businesses offer incentives in the form of in-store price cuts that aim to both reinforce the value credentials of the company and provide the opportunity to make a saving. Monetary promotions take many forms. As well as price discounting, coupons that are made available through a variety of channels are a very popular tactic. Rebates, where consumers can claim back money post-purchase, are complex but commonplace in certain categories. Using these forms of promotions effectively demands an intrinsic understanding of their characteristics, strengths, and weaknesses. This is increasingly vital as advances in consumer-facing technologies are changing the way monetary promotions—for example, coupons—are presented to shoppers. The insights offered will enable decision makers to take a more critical view of the use of these particular forms of sales promotions.

Discounting

Discounting lies at the heart of monetary promotions. It offers a reduction in price for a fixed period of time and is a core strategy in certain sectors. In the U.S. supermarket sector, for example, over 40 percent of sales are associated with some form of price reduction (Volpe and Li 2012). Discounting is used for a variety of reasons:

1. To create headline news on the high street
2. As a seasonal fixture in the promotional year
3. To correct or drive sales performance
4. To respond to a competitor threat
5. To encourage brand switching
6. To clear old or slow moving stock

It can also be used to stimulate interest from what have been termed *dormant customers*—those who are marginally interested, but who have price reservations (Mohammed 2010). Discounting or the *sale* still has vocal advocates (Eaton 2013); however, due to the thin margins in retail, it comes at a cost—to brand, margins, consumer perceptions, and price expectations. Discounting is therefore a *problem child* for the retail and consumer industries in particular for several key reasons.

Impact on Brand Perception and Brand Value

While all sales promotions ultimately seek to influence brand choice, it is important to consider the impact they may have on brand perceptions. Evidence suggests that while too much of any form of promotion might be a bad thing, the continued use of monetary promotions can be more damaging for brand equity in comparison to nonmonetary promotions (Yi and Yoo 2011). This is because continued discounting can act to potentially *cheapen* the brand.

Reference Pricing

Consumers are exposed to a wide range of product price information in their daily lives as shoppers. Because of this, they form a framework of mental norms, which help them to conceptualize what a normal or average price for a product is: a *reference price*. This helps consumers to identify a *good deal*, facilitating the assessment of a promotion's value and worth against everyday price experiences (Mazumdar, Raj, and Sinha 2005). When the shelf price is lower than the reference price, consumers anticipate a gain. If the shelf price is higher than the reference price, they perceive a loss (Fibich, Gavious, and Lowengart 2007). Reference prices may be influenced by internal and external experiences and stimuli: past shopping experiences, advertising, and promotional messaging; for example, Sinha and Prasad (2004). Continual, deep discounting may serve to decrease the reference price of a product in a consumer's mind; in the worst-case scenario, the discount price aligns with the reference price. This can compromise attempts to sell goods at full price in the future. In this situation, it can be argued, consumers have been successfully *trained* to wait for a price promotion or sale event as for them the discount price is the normal price. To combat this, research has shown that in the case of consumables, framing a deep discount in percentage terms may have a less negative impact on future price expectations (reference pricing) than when it is framed in terms of dollar or cent (DelVecchio, Krishnan, and Smith 2007).

Sales and Margin Issues

Selling a product at a discount will naturally affect average margins. For example, if you discount a product with a 40 percent initial margin by a rate of 30 percent, you would need a 300 percent increase in unit sales to realize the same margin dollars. As a promotional strategy, discounting carries a heavy load in terms of volume expectations and has been criticized across a range of retail markets and sectors for its negative impacts on profit and growth (Baker 2011; Cadman 2014; Townsend 2011). It has been identified as being especially detrimental to brands with high price points, low margins, and low short-term price responsiveness (Riggans 2012).

Although attractive to brand managers who are keen to make a quick hit impact, research from Holland analyzed four years of sales data from 560 consumer categories concluding that

> Although the total net short-term effects of price promotions are generally strong … they rarely exhibit persistent effects. Instead the effects dissipate over a time period lasting approximately 10 weeks on average, and their long-term impact is effectively zero. (Nijs et al. 2001, 1)

Promotional Big Dipper: Balancing the Before, During, and After

Businesses that engage in frequent promotional activity in the consumables sector should anticipate that purchase behavior may change not just during the promotional phase, but also before and after. This can result in promotional *dips*, which are the result of either consumers delaying a purchase in the anticipation of a promotion or sustaining themselves on the stockpiles acquired through promotional purchasing (Macé and Neslin 2004).

From a supplier perspective, it may be encouraging to know that price-based promotions can be effective in both stimulating demand in the promotional period and in encouraging brand switching. As with any promotion, it is important to remember that consumption is often finite, although some evidence of *consumption flexibility* has been noted— essentially people consuming more because they have more (Bell, Iyer, and Padmanabhan 2002).

Generally, although shoppers may buy a discounted product because of its attractive pricing, it does not mean they will revert to their usual consumption patterns in the medium term, relying instead on their stockpiles over the next purchase cycle. For example, because washing powder is reduced by 50 percent it does not mean that people do twice as much washing. An in-depth understanding of category purchasing and consumption behavior is therefore required.

In discretionary categories like wine, price promotions may encourage brand switching much more so than drive stockpiling (Panzone and Tiffin 2012). Shoppers may buy differently, but they may not buy more. This is a challenge for a multibrand supplier with largely homogenous price points as they need to be careful that they do not cannibalize base-line sales for a lesser margin. In addition, it is not beneficial to appeal to a consumer's motivation to stockpile if they are short in storage space. Research from the United States has shown that shoppers with limited storage space at home are not as responsive to stockpile-focused offers, simply because they do not have the space to store the bulk inventory offered (Bell and Hilber 2006).

Managing Discounting

As a key form of sales promotion, discounting can be used to illustrate the questions that promotional planners should ask when planning any campaign. Although discounting may be a default strategy for many businesses or an intrinsic part of the organization's marketing position, it should be carefully considered. Some basic, critical questions include the following:

Why are we discounting? What are the drivers behind the decision, and is discounting the best or the only option?

What are we discounting? A specific range, line, category, or department, or blanket discounting across the store? A new product or an existing product? For new product introductions, nonmonetary promotions may in fact be the best option as the novelty of the product means that shoppers do not need a financial incentive to purchase. Value adding (nonmonetary) rather than reducing price could therefore be seen as providing a more appropriate motivation (a *gain*, rather than a reduced *loss*), the logic of which is acknowledged in research (Lowe and Barnes 2012).

How deep are we discounting? The greater the discount, the greater the reference price impact, margin implications, and long-term baseline sales impact. Many retailers may in fact *over discount*. In some countries, discounts of 70 to 80 percent may be common, but this has been proposed to be much more than is required to elicit a purchase response. It may also cause the shopper to question the legitimacy of the offer, as well as making it tough for businesses to return to *normal* pricing due to the promotion/reference pricing divide (Marshall and Na 2000). There is a note of caution against going too hard and promoting too much of the same, with one commentator observing that "retail managers must be conscious not only of how deep they cut prices, but also the proportion of products in the same category that are offered on sale at one time" (Richards 2007, 88).

When are we discounting? What is the competitive or calendar *trigger* for the campaign? Are these logical and appropriate or merely inheritances from the past? For example, is the Founder's Day Sale still resonating with shoppers in the same way as it was 100 years ago? Are there additional or more relevant calendar sector-specific opportunities to consider?

How are we discounting? Discounts can take several forms including the following:

- Dollar/cents off
- Percentage off
- Was/now pricing (was $100, now only $75).

Research reveals that if the discount message is too confusing or complicated, shoppers may be put off trying to decipher the value behind the offer, as their *deal processing fluency* is compromised. They will therefore find the offer less attractive and may not be sufficiently motivated to do the math (Coulter and Roggeveen 2014). The key lesson is to ensure that the major economic benefit is clearly communicated, making use of round numbers and using logical multiples, for example, 10, 20, 30 percent.

How long are we discounting for? What is the rationale behind the duration of the campaign and at what point does sale data indicate that a point of promotional saturation has been reached?

How will we end the discount? Some shoppers leave things too late and visit the store only to find the price promotion has ended. One school of thought proposes that rather than go straight from low pricing, a strategy of steadily decreasing discounting (SDD) should be considered, concluding that "Managers should highly consider bringing the prices of their products back up to their original levels in steps instead of all at once to take advantage of higher future price expectations and greater anticipated inaction regret" (Tsiros and Hardesty 2010, 60).

How are we evaluating and measuring? What are the short-term and long-term impacts of the discount on sales and how are sales and profitability tracked? Discounting can impact not only sales and profit but also future purchasing behavior and brand perceptions; hence, the evaluation needs to consider financial as well as nonfinancial impacts.

These are important questions that are seldom comprehensively addressed. Without a clear and critical strategy, price-based promotion holds the biggest potential to damage brand, profit, and consumer sentiment more than any other form of promotional activity.

Coupons

Clip 'n' Save: A Family Favorite

The use of coupons has a long in history in many retail economies, most notable in the United States. Coupons provide an additional incentive to the consumer to try or buy and are most commonly monetary (discount-based) in nature, although they can be used to communicate other forms of promotional offers. They were most commonly presented to shoppers in the form of inserts or articles in newspapers, magazines, or newsletters and many families recall the keen *clipping* activities around the kitchen table. Coupon research spans several decades and has reported on a diverse range of interrelated factors including consumer preference and behavior, impact on brand perceptions, messaging, type and scale of benefit, redemption rates, and channels of distribution (Barat and Ye 2012). Businesses control the number of coupons printed and issued, with price reduction tending to be in the 20 to 30 percent range to motivate shoppers. As these campaigns offer the chance to get some face time with consumers, it is also worth considering the quality of the marketing messaging and the visual presentation, not just the size of the discount (Venkatesan and Farris 2012).

Redemption and Shopper Profile and Sentiment

Redemption rates are often very low, around 2 to 5 percent. Some researchers have suggested that in order to increase redemption rates, businesses should consider not offering a bigger discount, but present two mutually exclusive offers, that is, *choose $10 off your grocery bill* or *claim a free bottle of wine*. The argument is that shoppers will feel a greater sense of *missing out* when they reflect on two potential losses (even though only one could be redeemed) and will therefore be more likely to act (Weiss and Kivetz 2011). Coupons are most popular with value seeking commodity shoppers in categories like grocery and healthcare, with women often being the most enthusiastic adopters (Hill and Harmon 2009). However, with more men reported to be the primary shopper (Hill and Harmon 2007), it is important not to stereotype coupon users. The use of coupons may be sometimes associated with *cheapness* or *stinginess*, creating potential social stigma for users (Argo and Main 2008). This may incline some consumers not to redeem a voucher even if it is a good deal, as they would prefer to avoid this stigma, valuing a social goal over an economic benefit (Ashworth, Darke, and Schaller 2005). Having a separate queue for coupon users, or calling a manager or supervisor to publically authenticate a coupon discount, might not be good for business in some parts of town!

Coupons and New Technologies

Couponing has also moved both online and into the mobile channel. Research from Austria shows that for the mobile channel (especially for value seeking shoppers), simplicity is the key, with managers needing to focus on the ease of process, educating shoppers along the way. They also need to avoid *spamming* shoppers, and be clear about how privacy will be respected (Dickinger and Kleijnen 2008).

The mobile channel can be used in different ways, for example, to send a coupon, to encourage the customer to ring and reserve a special priced item, or to direct them to follow a hyperlink. Emergent *geo-fencing* technologies means that when potential customers enter a predetermined geographical perimeter (e.g., a sports arena or a ski resort), they can receive promotional messaging from preferred retailers that can include mobile coupons (*Effective Sales Promotion: Playing to Win over the Customer* 2014).

Research from Japan suggests that it is important to use the method of engagement most relevant to the specific customer, highlighting the need to segment and target messages not just on the basis of income, age, or geography, but also on mobile channel preference (Kondo and Nakahara 2007).

Social Couponing

The internet has facilitated the growth of the social group-based promotional discount, for example, Groupon and Living Social. The Groupon business model presents followers with one major deal per day at a discounted price. If a specified number of signups is secured, the discount becomes available to all. The revenue from the voucher sale is shared between Groupon and the promotion provider.

While advantageous for the mobile service provider and the customer, the potential benefits to a retailer may be compromised by poor planning and inadequate forecasting. This may lead to disastrous consequences if the redemption rates of purchased vouchers are higher than anticipated. This can cause fulfilment problems due to unmanageable demand as a result of huge sales volumes. It may mean that higher staff and establishment costs are incurred, reducing margins. Retailers need to be aware that future sales may be affected as consumers stockpile at the reduced price.

Beyond Redemption: Retailer Customized Couponing

Aligned to the growth in the use of loyalty programs and the demographic and purchase history data that can be gathered, couponing has become less of a mass mail out exercise and more of a targeted initiative. Shoppers can now receive coupons and special offers considered to be more relevant to them. These are called *retailer customized coupon* campaigns and are usually focused at the top tier of shoppers in the database. Research from the United States revealed that mere exposure to customized coupon campaigns can increase a customer's net worth, meaning they may be motivated to shop more intensely whether or not they actually redeem. This has important implications for campaign managers, as the traditional measure of a coupon campaign is often solely the redemption rate (Venkatesan and Farris 2012).

Evaluating Coupon Performance

Coupon campaigns present decision makers with many design choices, including discount level, benefit framing (dollar or percentage) timing and duration, segmentation, and channel. Evaluation, however, often focuses on a single measure—redemption rates—with claims made that managers do not have adequate evaluation models or processes in place (Wei 2007). Managers are therefore encouraged to look beyond redemption and take note of other positive metrics that may be attributed to the coupon initiative. They are encouraged to consider factors including customer satisfaction, change in average invoice value, visit frequency, associated product sale and overall value perception, and well as conducting demographic analysis on exactly who does the redeeming.

Coupons are a well tried and tested option for putting purchasing power in the hands of consumers. As such, they are among the most prominent examples of front-loaded promotional offers. They also share shelf space with a rear-loaded relative—*rebates*. As these two options are frequently compared, it is worthwhile exploring the similarities and differences.

Rebates

Buy Now, Save Later

Rebates differ from coupons in that rather than providing an upfront incentive to buy, consumers—having purchased a product at the advertised price—apply to the manufacturer or retailer for a partial refund. This requires extra effort on the part of the consumer and in effect delays the receipt of the benefit. Because of the administration required, rebates are more suitable for higher ticket price goods where more substantial sums are involved, compared with coupons many of which only offer low dollar or sometimes only cents savings. In the United States, they are an important marketing tool for expensive consumer durables like automobiles, with an estimated U.S. $3 billion paid out in 2006 (Bruce, Desai, and Staelin 2006). On face value, it looks like the vendor has the upper hand in relation to rebates. Full price can be charged for a product, with the advertised saving only being reimbursed when the claim process is completed. Some shoppers may have reservations about whether the rebate will actually be paid, or be concerned about the time lag between application and receipt, so this option may be less attractive to risk-averse shoppers who like their savings in real time.

Conditional Love

Rebates can be offered as conditional incentives, for example, in product categories where seasonality may significantly affect purchase behavior and subsequent product usage. One source reviewed cites the example of a Canadian snowmobile manufacturer who offered a cash rebate if snowfall in 44 states was below the previous three-year average. Sales grew by 38 percent, with the promotion insured through a financial product known as a *weather derivative* (Gao, Demirag, and Chen 2012).

Nonredemption: Slippage

Only 40 percent of rebates are claimed (an effect called *slippage*), essentially reducing the overall cost of the promotion compared to regular discounting or couponing (Qiang and Moorthy 2007). There are many reasons why consumers may not redeem. They may be forgetful, value the potential saving less over time, find the process too hard and therefore not worthwhile, or they may simply not be deal prone shoppers (Choi, Kissan, and Lemieux 2010). The goal of rebates is however to motivate shoppers to purchase with the rebate in mind. The rebate structure and process management should therefore serve to encourage not dissuade. Several factors have been proposed that could make rebates more appealing including easy-to-complete forms, rebate payment tracking (online or via a toll free number), short payback time (circa two months), and the use of online redemption rather than paper-based tools (Ong 2008).

Manufacturer Rebates

Another application of rebates involves manufacturers paying a cash sum to a retailer, often as part of a trading agreement that prevents the business selling competitor products (exclusivity). In this way, rebates act to compensate for the opportunity cost of lost sales (Erutku 2006). Sometimes, manufacturers offer incentives to both the business and to the end consumer (Demirag et al. 2010).

Legal Complexities

In the United States rebates are big business. In line with other promotional and marketing strategies, they have attracted the attention of legislators and those who offer rebates must do so within legal parameters. There is concern, for example, about product prices being presented, which include the potential rebate but do not clearly identify that a rebate needs to be applied for. Diverse federal and state laws exist relating to rebates, meaning that sellers and manufacturers need to be competent in legal interpretation and also in service contract fulfilment. These are significant managerial issues both for reasons of compliance and due to a huge increase reported in customer complaints relating to rebates (Pechmann and Silk 2013).

Although commonplace, monetary promotions have their limitations. Many businesses therefore like to consider other forms of promotion, which although still incurring a cost do not necessarily depend on playing the *price game*. This illustrates a shift toward nonmonetary promotional strategies (Cooper 2011), the main forms of which will now be explored in the following chapters.

Chapter Highlights

- Monetary promotions take many forms including discounting, couponing, and rebates.
- Excessive discounting can have negative implications for brand and price perceptions.
- Monetary discounts can adversely impact margins.
- A clear rational and strategy is needed when using monetary promotions to minimize potentially damaging consequences.
- New technologies are changing the way monetary promotions are presented to consumers.
- Evolutions in social media have presented new consumers to take advantage of group buying incentives.

CHAPTER 5

Nonmonetary Sales Promotions

Introduction

The previous chapter explored the major forms of monetary promotions. This chapter defines and discusses nonmonetary promotions as an alternative to price-based promotions. There are several popular forms of nonmonetary promotion that center on adding value to a purchase rather than discounting price. We highlight the specific characteristics of these types of promotion and reveal key research insights relating to their use, design, and application. At a time when increasing consumer skepticism toward sales promotions is a very real consideration for decision makers, we also review the benefits of both monetary and nonmonetary promotions within the promotional mix.

What Are Nonmonetary Promotions?

Nonmonetary promotions do not discount price, but instead offer added value in the form of a free gift, a bonus size product, a discount on a further unit purchase, or a sweepstake (competition) entry. Many forms of nonmonetary promotions are sometimes referred to collectively as *premium promotions*. By employing nonmonetary promotions, margins are preserved and the sometimes negative associations relating to discounting are avoided. These promotions still incur costs based on the nature of the reward or incentive offered. As with a price-based promotion, the benefits offered to the consumer may be large or small, but unlike a discount the reward may be certain (guaranteed as a result of purchase) or uncertain (i.e., a sweepstake entry that offers the chance to enter and win a prize). While discounting offers utilitarian (functional) benefits, some nonmonetary promotions can be perceived as appealing to hedonic (pleasure-seeking) motivations, especially those with an engagement, education, fun, or challenge aspect included. When compared to highly visible price discounting, nonprice promotions are often considered less well researched (Liao 2006). While discounting options may be fairly limited, nonmonetary promotions by contrast offer more in the way of choice, scope, and messaging.

Bonus Packs—Buy One Get One Free

The use of bonus-sized packs (200 ml for the price of 150 ml), or the offer of buy one get one free (BOGOF) are popular forms of sales promotion in household goods categories. Rather than offering a price discount, the benefit centers on offering a quantity advantage of the same—or a related—product. Rather than *50 percent off*, these promotions are often framed as *100 percent more*. How these promotions are presented, the magnitude of the offer, and how consumers interpret and evaluate the added value will, of course, determine their success (Chen et al. 2012). They often leave full price largely intact. They can also be a valuable way to pass on surplus or soon to be discontinued product to shoppers with a stockpiling and value-seeking mentality. They therefore offer manufacturing, supply chain, and demand smoothing advantages. This form of promotion can also impact competitor sales and prevent brand switching. They have also attracted some criticism, centering on creating waste, encouraging bad eating habits and overconsumption and the potential to devalue brands through overuse. Whether bonus packs are preferred over discounts may depend on the aptitude of the organization in modeling and comparing relative campaign costs. As this form of promotion involves manufacturing, distribution, and marketing skills, those responsible for promotion planning are encouraged to take a more holistic approach to cost calculation and campaign decision making (Geurreiro et al. 2004).

Free Gift with Purchase

Free gifts are another form of value-adding sales promotion. They are a common strategy in highly brand-sensitive categories including cosmetics and home electronics where discounting the brand is often actively avoided. The free gift may be in the form of a complimentary product from the brand stable or from a different brand, category, or supplier. Once again, it is all down to interpretation and perception on the part of the consumer, with researchers providing some valuable points of consideration. Shoppers may undervalue the gift simply because it is free. They may also mentally devalue the category from which the gift came. Conversely, they may attribute a higher value to a gift if it is offered by a more prestigious brand. As the product has been given away, it is also unlikely the shopper will need to buy it, so standalone sales of the gifted item may suffer (Raghubir 2004). These factors relate to what has been termed a *spillover* effect (Tseng, Lou, and Bei 2009) and illustrate how the wider effects of individual promotions need to be considered. Offering a mystery gift with purchase may be problematic. Not telling the consumer what the free gift is can have two possible effects—it can turn off risk-adverse shoppers due to the inherent risk of not knowing, or it can entice those who enjoy a degree of mystery with an element of fun (Laran and Tsiros 2013). Finally, for those who may miss out on the free gift offer, negative emotions caused by a sense of regret may be evident (Liu, Cheng, and Ni 2011). Overall, it is important for business to consider both the advantages of gift giving as well as the potential drawbacks through data analysis and consumer research.

Bundling

Sharing similarities with bonus pack promotions is a technique referred to as product *bundling*. Bundling involves multiple items being offered for sale together with some form of extra value incentive offered. The value may be communicated in the form of a price advantage or through the offer of a free (and sometimes unique) product. Bundling can create an immediate sense of appeal, especially if the bundle price is promoted against the total costs of the products if they were to be purchased separately. If you are feeling hungry, a good example of bundling is the regular meal deals offered at McDonalds: You can buy any of the products separately, although there is a value advantage in taking the bundle offer. Potential image problems may be attributed to bundling of fast food, via the *combo* approach, for example, with the increase in calorific intake or the offer only of soft drinks with no healthy alternative being a cause for concern. Customers may negate these consequences though, perceiving the ease of ordering (*meal 1 please*) as a benefit in itself (Shibin, Parker, and Nakamoto 2007). Examples are also found in the music industry, especially in the online selling space where consumers may take advantage of an offer to bundle music tracks or albums from their favorite artists (Bodily and Mohammed 2006).

Consumers often have reservations about bundle deals. They can find the deal too hard to evaluate asking "is this really a better deal than buying the individual items elsewhere?" They may also not value some items included in the bundle and see them as irrelevant or surplus to requirements. Research has revealed that shoppers may have reservations about the quality of the value-adding bundled product and can be wary of its full price value due to its role as the loss leader component (Shibin, Parker, and Nakamoto 2007). For events and leisure marketers, bundling may be a good way to assemble an attractive one-price package that covers diverse elements. The question of redemption is again raised, with some research indicating that consumers may be more likely to forgo a bundle component than if they had bought the event and attraction tickets individually (Soman and Gourville 2001). As an alternative to single-price bundling, it has been suggested that firms may consider presenting a reduced price for each bundle item, if purchased together (Yadav and Monroe 1993). They may serve to attract not just pure bundle shoppers, but also those who were interested in any of the components individually. It has also been proposed that bundling a new, innovative, and untried product with a familiar, established item may encourage purchase likelihood and reduce the risk that is associated with the purchase of the unfamiliar item (Harris 1997; Sarin, Sego, and Chanvarasuth 2003).

In discount-driven times, bundling may be seen as a way that powerful brands can differentiate themselves (Chung, Lin, and Hu 2013), creating a unique market offer with inherent category strengths and product synergies.

Those familiar with online music buying (e.g., iTunes) will also be familiar with the practice of *unbundling*, for example, where an album is broken down into separate tracks, and subsequently offered for sale

(Chiambaretto and Dumez 2012). This is the opposite of the *meal deal* approach, and shoppers may pay more per unit, but ultimately get exactly what they want.

Sampling

In competitive consumer environments, many retailers and suppliers seek to influence and motivate potentially undecided or hesitant consumers through the active promotion of products through sampling. This is a familiar part of the supermarket and department store landscape and is a good way to get products off the shelf and into the customers' hands. Sampling can also take to the streets or may involve direct mailing or even online avenues. In the software sector, sampling involves the use of freeware or trial ware (Lee and Tan 2013). Sampling is strongly associated with experiential marketing (that which engages a range of senses) and aims to involve the target consumer tacitly and tangibly with the product. As a consequence, sampling may also include a theatrical or event element to build excitement and interest. This may be achieved through the use of special displays, custom vehicles, attractive models, or interactive technologies. Sampling may also be linked to other forms of incentive, for example, a price reduction or a bonus offer. Sampling in all its forms has been used widely in consumer markets and the broad consensus is that it is a powerful way to drive sales. It fulfills a variety of roles, including the following:

- Raising brand awareness
- Encouraging new product trial
- Attracting new consumers
- Assisting with the demonstration of a multi-stage or system application (e.g., a two-stage skin care process)
- Helping with brand or product repositioning (Sherwood 2006)

For these reasons, companies from all sectors spend billions of dollars per annum on sampling initiatives. Sampling can shape consumer behavior in two ways: encouraging immediate purchase and developing longer-term goodwill (Heiman et al. 2001). Therefore, as well as being a powerful and flexible way to introduce a new product, it can also assist longer-term brand goals. In addition, sampling can also be an effective method to re-introduce familiar brand products to new audiences.

Sampling presents consumers with the chance to experience a new product with no attendant risk. In the case of online music retailing, it has been proposed that offering samples to potential consumers may help mitigate the effects of contradictory reviews, for example (Hu et al. 2010). In the case of food sampling in particular, it can also be seen as a form of reward or treat—something to break the monotony of a regular trip around the supermarket. It can also motivate shoppers to engage in more hedonistic shopping activities, providing you do not give them too much of a good thing and thereby fully satiate their appetite (Wadhwa, Shiv, and Nowlis 2006)! In discerning, brand-driven sectors like beauty, just because a sample is free, should not mean it is cheap. This may be the only chance to change the buying habits of a lifetime and encourage the shopper to switch brands. Where sampling is concerned, first impressions count. Managers are encouraged to give thought and attention to packaging design and quality, as well as consider ways in which the packaging itself can be used to create interest and engagement (Penning 2013).

The expansion of social media has opened new frontiers for the use of sampling. Rather than being a hit or miss affair, samples can be targeted at those who show an active interest in an organization's social media sites, and they can be used to encourage more people to subscribe in return for a free sample. Strong networkers, that is, those with the highest density of connections, can also be targeted as *word of web* brand champions and product advocates, leveraging *social contagion* (Schlereth et al. 2013).

Embedded Premiums

An embedded premium is one in which the benefits accrue to a social cause or charity. They offer a different and potentially more altruistic benefit and often require no additional action on behalf of the consumer. They may be framed as: "for every product purchased, $1.00 will be donated to charity x," for example. This form of promotion offers some distinct potential advantages for brands (Henderson and Arora 2010):

1. Avoidance of the negative association and margin implications associated with discounting.
2. Provides the opportunity for a brand to make a synergistic connection with a worthwhile cause, especially one which can be seen to reflect the brand focus, market position, or consumer demographic.
3. It can generate a feel-good factor for shoppers, as their purchase contributes to a worthwhile cause.
4. There is potential to apply premium price strategies, with shoppers perhaps willing to pay more for the opportunity to *do good* through their purchase.
5. It may enable less established or *challenger* brands to benefit by association with a known charitable entity.
6. The potential to actively encourage brand switching.

Overall, it has been proposed, a comparatively small benefit can be more effective than offering the equivalent benefit in discount or coupon form (Henderson and Arora 2010). This is because a consumer may place a higher mental value on the donation, in comparison to the cost saving.

Competitions, Sweepstakes, and Contests

Winning Entry

Sales promotions based on competitions, contests, promotional games, or sweepstakes present consumers with the chance to win a prize as a result of engagement. They are commonly employed by leading consumer brands and the investment can be considerable. In the United States, for example, in 2008, $1.86 billion was spent on these initiatives by a range of organizations as part of their sales promotion agenda (Johannes 2008). Qualifying to enter one of these campaigns may involve purchase, product trial, store visitation, viewing an online advertisement, getting a code word from a magazine, agreeing to receive a newsletter, or completing a survey providing details or information. Familiar to most is providing a creative answer to a *25 words or less* question. Whether or not purchase is required, these efforts can be considered a cost of entry, or what is termed *consideration* (Stanley 2003). Popular prizes range from cash, cars, and holidays to free products and *money can't buy* experiences. These campaigns are popular and highly visible in-store and online through websites and have also evolved to take advantage of the mobile channel and social media space in more recent years. There is a strong community of consumers who actively and enthusiastically enter these promotions. Referred to as *compers*, or less attractively *prize pigs*, they interact through forums and virtual networks sharing competition information, code words, winning strategies, and celebrate each other's wins.

Advantages

Several key advantages for these campaigns have been identified. These include brand repositioning, increasing consumer awareness, creating impact at point of sale, increasing awareness of range, heightening in-store interest, and encouraging brand switching (Peattie, Peattie, and Emafo 1997). They can also inject a hedonic element of fun, chance, or gaming into the otherwise utilitarian price-centered promotional landscape. It is also relevant to consider their role in relation to customer relationship management (CRM). A detailed customer database is increasingly important for effective marketing. Competitions, sweepstakes, and contests are an effective means by which relevant consumer information can be collected as part of the entry process.

Design Parameters

On the face of it, competitions, sweepstakes, and contests look simple. In reality, managers are faced with an array of design choices. The extensive research conducted into these campaigns for this book revealed four main decision fields that present challenges to decision makers:

1. Campaign profile: What are the conditions of entry and the rules of the game?
2. Marketing channels: How and where will the campaign be presented to consumers?

3. Prize structure: How are winners selected: chance or luck? What is the nature of the prize: cars, cash, holidays? What is the prize dispersion: single winner, few winners, multiple winners?

4. Timing and duration: When will the promotion run and for how long?

It is important to consider these design factors against the objectives established for the campaign. For example, designing a competition with the goal of increasing sales without including a purchase clause in the terms and conditions will be unlikely to succeed as consumers can enter whether or not they make a purchase.

Legal Considerations

Competitions, sweepstakes, and contests as well as being sales promotion tools also share features more commonly found in the gaming or gambling arenas. As a consequence, campaign planners need to comply with not only consumer law but with national and state gaming legislation. This can dictate entry criteria, the nature of any consideration, costs of entry, and the value and nature of the prize. It is common for this form of legislation to be state specific, so a national campaign may require multiple state permits. As a result of this complexity and to avoid costly fines, many organizations chose to employ the services of lawyers or promotional agencies who specialize in managing the legalities, operation, and management of these campaigns.

Overall, they offer the consumer an engaging, attractive, and enjoyable promotional opportunity. Despite their popularity they remain largely under-researched.

Monetary or Nonmonetary: Which Is Best?

Having explored the diverse forms of monetary and nonmonetary promotions, it is clear that both can offer different potential advantages. Consumer-facing organizations use monetary and nonmonetary promotions in varying proportions and for diverse reasons. Supermarket retailing, for example, is heavily price and value focused and discounting and the use of coupons, for example, is commonplace all year round. Department stores may discount at key times of the year only, supplementing this with more creative initiatives like sampling and BOGOF campaigns. Retailers of electrical products will often focus on discounting, but due to the higher ticket price, price visibility, and the low margins associated with their products they may also rely on rebates to close the deal.

Obviously, there is no one answer to the question *which is best*. Research in the field provides some interesting food for thought, relating to consumer perceptions, benefit levels, and the most appropriate choice of promotional tool (Palazon and Delgado-Ballester 2009). For example, at a moderate level of promotional benefit, there may be little or no difference in consumer perceptions between the relative advantages of a monetary versus a nonmonetary promotion. At low-benefit levels, it seems that a dollar spend on a nonmonetary promotion will be more effective than an equivalent investment in discounting. With a high promotional benefit, consumers seem to value the discount offer more. For managers who may be creatures of habit when it comes to promotional choice, it is worth considering that discounting may not be the only option for all occasions or price points. Sector dynamics, market position, and customer expectations will, however, ultimately shape the final profile of the campaigns adopted.

Keep it Real

With prices changing all the time, and a glut of unbeatable offers confronting shoppers every day, it is not surprising that a degree of skepticism and cynicism is to be expected, with claims like *lowest ever prices* and *never to be repeated offer* often raising suspicions. Consumer skepticism toward such sales promotions is revealed to have a detrimental impact on purchase intentions as well as causing shoppers to downplay the perceived level of benefit (de Pechpeyrou and Odou 2012). Collectively, businesses and brands must take responsibility for this, as the industry continually drives promotional activity with sometimes seemingly wild claims. Despite the wide choices available to managers, discounting in particular remains prevalent and it has also been called the *new retail reality* (Knight 2012). This may be because promotional alternatives are not explored in enough detail by those who make campaign decisions through their planning activities. Hence, having explored these major monetary and nonmonetary options, we now turn our attention to the sales promotion planning process as the next stage in our journey.

Chapter Highlights

- Nonmonetary promotions focus on adding value rather than reducing price.
- This form of promotion is often referred to as a *premium promotion*.
- Major forms include BOGOF, free gifts, bundling, sample, embedded premiums, and competitions.
- Each form of nonmonetary promotion offers specific benefits and advantages to the retailer.
- There is still active debate on the most effective combination of monetary and nonmonetary promotions.
- Embedded premiums are a specific from of sales promotion with not-for-profit or charity applications.

CHAPTER 6

Sales Promotion Decision Making: Processes and Influences

In previous decades, marketing managers often failed to recognise the importance of co-ordinating and integrating the promotion mix as the various elements were planned and managed separately, often by different people with different objectives, budgets, and views of the market. (Stewart and Gallen 1998, 557)

Introduction

Every sales promotion campaign will be the result of an applied management process, whether formally defined or informally negotiated. These processes are often unique to an organization's market position and culture, and they will be shaped by a number of factors. In this chapter, we define the core stages in the decision-making process and discuss the major influences—internal and external—that can shape decisions. This provides a platform upon which the reader can begin to critically consider decision-making approaches within their own organization. The chapter also establishes a basis for the cross-case comparison presented later in the book.

Decisions, Decisions

Sales promotion decision makers face some unique challenges. They have to assess the overall competitive position and the brand values of the organization and develop a suite of promotional initiatives that support business goals relating to sales, profit, category performance, inventory management and stock holding, differentiation, and consumer satisfaction. Their job is made more difficult because dynamic variables like seasonality, competitor activity, new product launches, internal preferences, and budget constraints will all need to be accommodated in the decision-making process. They have to be both proactive and reactive, developing solid promotional foundations and accommodating tactical demands. Despite these complexities, they must review and analyze the information and data available to them, applying experience and expertise to develop promotional strategies necessary to deliver the best possible return on investment—both short term and long term.

Sales Promotions: What Are the Big Questions?

The specific decisions that managers make in relation to sales promotions are often complex and wide ranging, but essentially seek to address the following questions:

Objective setting: What are the specific and measurable aims of the promotional strategy?

Budget and resource allocation: How much is allocated to sales promotions within the marketing mix?

Options: Which forms of promotion are most suitable in fulfilling stated objectives?

Promotional mix: How are diverse promotional options combined to create a coherent and synergistic mix over the calendar year?

Campaign design: How are specific campaigns themed, marketed, and operationalized?

Timing, duration, scheduling, and frequency: When are promotions scheduled and why? How are multiple promotions managed and coordinated over time to balance the offer and to avoid customer confusion and *promotion fatigue*.

Agency involvement: Are sales promotions designed and managed in-house, or are specialist agencies employed for some or all of the campaign stages?

Stakeholder involvement: What degree of feedback and engagement is sought from stakeholders in relation to the promotional offer, for example, other head office departments, store managers, or franchisees?

Supplier partnership: Are suppliers involved in campaign decision making, and how are diverse supplier-led promotions assessed and coordinated?

Implementation: Who is responsible for campaign activation and management? How is overall control coordinated in circumstances where different parts of the business may be responsible for different aspects of the campaign at different stages?

Evaluation: What measures are used to assess the impact of the campaign against the stated objectives and how are learnings shared and incorporated in future campaigns?

Processes and Influences at Work

Every organization is unique in terms of its culture, structure, market position, and management style. This also extends to decision making in all business areas, including marketing advertising and sales promotion planning. Organizations have their own *ways of doing things*, for example. Some may have a high dependency on hard facts and data to guide decisions. Others may take a more intuitive and experience-based approach. Some leave decision making to the marketers, while others encourage a more collaborative and consultative approach, taking many view points and opinions into account from stakeholders. What is certain is that all businesses adopt some form of decision-making *process* that results in decisions being made. This process may be formal or informal and intuitive or data-driven. The specific process will also be subject to internal and external forces or *influences* that act to shape the nature and focus of the decisions taken.

Decision-Making Process in the Real World

Sales promotion planning often involves complex negotiations between organizational divisions and departments, manufacturers, suppliers, and stakeholders. Not surprisingly, the quality of the planning process undertaken has been identified by experts as a critical factor in determining the future use (and success of) any promotional initiative (Stewart and Gallen 1998). In essence, good planning will increase the chances of a successful campaign, while inefficient planning will likely result in disappointing results, leading to the effectiveness of sales promotions being questioned by those involved or affected.

The impact that decisions taken by management have upon the nature and effectiveness of a given sales promotion have been considered since the swinging 1960s (Weber 1963). Even back then, the potentially negative impacts that management approach and organizational culture could have were noted. To consolidate understanding, it is important to explore what is known about the sales promotion planning process and understand the fundamentals of the stages involved in delivering a successful campaign considering both theory and practice in the field.

Sales Promotions: Theory–Practice Interface

"Few areas of marketing exhibit a greater disparity between theory and practice than sales promotion" (Gaidis and Cross 1987, 67).

Perhaps not surprisingly, like marketing and advertising, the field of sales promotion decision making also seems to be one where a theory–practice divide is evident. In the supermarket industry in New Zealand, for example, it has been proposed that "a coherent system for decision making is lacking" (Simpson 2006, 225).

Diverse frameworks and models have been proposed to help managers to develop more effective processes and optimize promotional effectiveness. These are found readily in textbooks and journals, often taking the form of flowcharts or checklists, populated with decision stages and key questions that the promotional planner is encouraged to ask and answer at each stage.

Others have framed their thinking around the sales promotion decision factors that managers have to address in their planning processes (Raghubir, Inman, and Grande 2004). The model in this case considered five key design fields (choice of product to promote, choice of target segment, type of promotion and design, promotion pattern intensity, and communication), again identifying some relatively common-sense decision stages that managers are encouraged to follow.

The more scientifically minded advocate the use of *decision support systems* (more metrics, data, and analytics driven) to fill a perceived void in the planning process (Silva-Risso, Bucklin, and Morrison 1999). Some have proposed frameworks that center on decision stages that focus on stages of consumer engagement and response (Gaidis and Cross 1987). It is, however, commonly identified that promotional planning is neither art nor science, but a combination of the two (Dhebar, Neslin, and Quelch 1987), the success of which relies heavily on the experience of decision makers and their ability to read the market and propose the best solution.

As can be seen, there is no clear consensus on what could be considered a standard or generic model or framework that can be universally applied to the discussion of sales promotions, as there is, for example, in the case of the Boston Consulting Group's 4Ps of marketing decision making, familiar to many. It often seems that the more specific a model or paradigm is, the less applicable it is. The combined work of business writers, consultants, systems developers, and functional decision makers over recent decades has, if nothing else, created a diversity of opinion.

Model Answer

In order to structure our thinking, a pragmatic model has been developed that aims to synthesize the diverse views on the stages of the planning process. This provides common ground for discussion and analysis. This model is one in which the stages of which are recognizable to all, even if in practice not all the process stages are completed, nor followed in the order specified. This model is shown in Figure 6.1.

Exploring the Process Stages

1. *Aims.* An overall *big picture* of the role of sales promotions in supporting business goals is developed, drawn from the direction provided in the annual marketing plan.

2. *Resources.* The amount of funding and resources available for sales promotions within the marketing and advertising budget needs to be identified. This may change over time as business circumstances evolve, but planners must start with a clear picture on the likely resources at their disposal to facilitate seasonal or annualized budgeting.

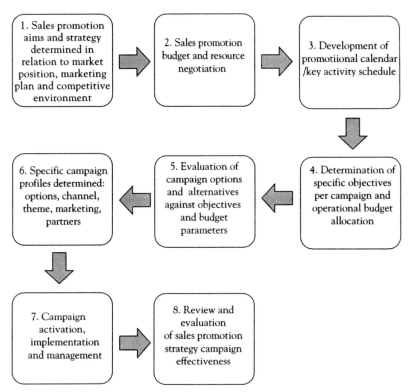

Figure 6.1 The stages of sales promotion planning

3. *Activity planning.* Over the course of the business year, a promotional plan needs to be drafted and refined, which identifies the key times where promotional activity will have the greatest impact. It should also present a schedule of proposed activity that both capitalizes on opportunity and avoids promotional bottlenecks and lengthy periods of inactivity.

4. *Objective setting.* For every campaign, clear objectives need to be determined, identifying the specific goals that each campaign is intended to achieve. These may relate to brand or product awareness, sales, profit, volume, or product lifecycle leverage. Without a clear idea of what the promotion is intended to achieve, the subsequent campaign design exercises and the evaluation of effectiveness is compromised and any evaluation exercises will be both confused and potentially ineffective.

5. *Modeling and evaluation of alternatives.* With clear promotional objectives established, it is important to acknowledge that there may be more than one way to achieve these goals. This is a critical step in the planning cycle, as it is easy to default to tried-and-tested old favorites, rather than explore fresh alternatives.

6. *Campaign specifics.* After considering possible alternatives, decisions need to be made on the specifics of campaign profiles. Which form of promotion will be used to best achieve the particular campaign objectives? Which channels will the promotion occupy and how will the promotion be themed and communicated to consumers? Will the campaign involve external partners and service providers, for example, suppliers, legal experts, and marketing agencies?

7. *Management and implementation.* Responsibility for campaign activation will need to be delegated. In some cases, organizations outsource some or all of their promotional campaign management to third parties, while in other cases this remains an internal responsibility.

8. *Evaluation.* With clear objectives established for each campaign, it is important to conduct review and evaluation exercises to determine how successful the promotion was in fulfilling these objectives. Evaluation may be based on a limited number of factors, for example, short-term sales lift, or may be more comprehensive and extensive, including short- and long-term sales modification, brand perception, cross-category impact, customer reaction, shopper behavior, and stakeholder satisfaction.

Diversity in Decision Making

This process model presents distinct decision stages recognizable to the majority of decision makers with responsibility for sales promotions. It therefore provides a solid platform to discuss what could, should, and does happen in the day-to-day life of professionals. Diverse, company-specific processes will mean that not all stages may be followed in the specified order and the level of rigor, detail, and analysis applied at each stage may also vary. The reason that there is such diversity in decision making is twofold. First, because there is no common agreement on the optimal process, practices within organizations have evolved along different paths, often blending history, experience, and common practice. Second—and significant—is that all decisions are subject to the forces of cultural and competitive influences, both internal and external and it is important to acknowledge and define these potential sources of influence.

Under the Influence

Whichever process or method is used by an organization, whether analytics and systems driven or more organic and informal, it is important to maintain a keen awareness of the potential sources of influence that will shape outcomes. Different markets, competitive conditions, ownership, and operating structures and business cultures will all influence how decisions are made. Sometimes these influences are overt, but sometimes they may be more subtle and less obvious in their impact. Unless we acknowledge the factors that shape our decisions, it is hard to take a critical and objective look at why we do what we do. This is just as true for sales promotion planning as it is for all other management decision fields.

Influences on Promotional Planning

Some influences, such as management experience, market knowledge, and hard data, can have a positive and beneficial effect. Sometimes however they may negatively impact campaign effectiveness, for example, if the culture of the business is risk averse, or if a small number of powerful stakeholders get the final say regardless of their competence in the field. These influences will vary in nature and significance between businesses. They should nevertheless be recognized to ensure that management decisions are optimized, not compromised. The sources of influence may be either *external* or *internal* in origin. Our research identified some major sources that practitioners should be aware of (Table 6.1).

External Influences

Trading Environment

While strategic marketing develops long-term relationships with consumers, sales promotions are—as identified—short-term response tools.

Table 6.1 External and internal influences on decision making

Sales promotion decision influences	
External influence factors	**Internal influence factors**
1. Trading environment	1. Market and brand position
2. Competitor activity	2. Marketing plan focus and direction
3. Seasonality: markets, categories,	agenda and direction
products	3. Category and product sales, market
4. Supplier relationships and partnerships	share, and margin targets
5. Stakeholder expectations: contractual,	4. Experience and preferences of decision
service, and legal obligations	makers
6. Marketing agency contribution	5. Budget allocation methods
	6. Organizational structure and internal
	stakeholder dynamics
	7. Campaign evaluation

That does not mean that businesses cannot plan their sales promotions strategies ahead of time and many develop a detailed promotional calendar extending a full 12 months in advance. However, changes in the trading environment, such as a rise in interest rates, a slowdown in consumer spending, increased jobless figures, or concern about the global economy can influence the nature, depth, and frequency of sales promotions required to achieve sales goals as anticipated spending patterns change. In times of economic downturn, for example, many retailers in discretionary or luxury sectors may find that sales decline as shoppers abstain from purchasing, or seek cheaper alternatives. They will have to work harder to try to engage consumers with more promotions and special offers as a consequence. In the supermarket sector, many players find themselves having to promote value rather than location, range, or convenience as their key message to the market. Everyday low pricing (EDLP) price rollbacks and *feed a family for less than $10* campaigns are commonplace in promotional messaging. This is because midmarket players like Tesco and Sainsbury's (UK) and Coles and Woolworths (Australia) are losing ground to hard discounters like Aldi, Lidl, Netto, and Costco. Department stores are susceptible to falls in consumer confidence and declines in discretionary spending, so when the going gets tough additional sales and heavy discounting may be introduced even if it potentially comprises brand values.

Competitor Activity

It is always necessary to keep a close eye on the competition. The strategies and actions of competitors can influence promotional decision making quite significantly. Deeper and more widespread discounting may be required, which may not have been anticipated when promotional plans were first proposed. New campaign messaging may have to be developed to counter a strong brand offensive or minimize the impact of a new market entrant. Those responsible for sales promotions may find themselves reacting to rapidly changing competitive circumstances, introducing new campaigns or amending planned campaigns at relatively short notice as part of the planning process to help the business defend its position. This is most evident in the case of *price wars*, for example. These are a common feature of the supermarket sector where one retailer seeks to aggressively demonstrate their value credentials to consumers in key staple goods categories like bread and milk through deep discounting or *loss leader* tactics.

Seasonality: Markets, Categories, Products

Some businesses plan their inventory purchasing and sales forecasts with a strong focus on the changing seasons, from a trend, event, or climate perspective. The fashion retailing industry is one that drives its marketing and promotional activities around spring, summer, autumn, and winter collections and global fashion *catwalk* events. It is common to see end of season sales, followed by new season launches or high-profile fashion event associations. Sporting goods retailers also plan their category promotions around the sporting calendar and the key seasons and events in the local, national, or international sporting world. When a particular sports season commences, there is an abundance of promotional activity aimed at motivating shoppers to refresh their clothing and equipment at key times of the year. Leisure, recreation, and outdoors goods retailers also have to accommodate peak buying times for their products at different times of the year and will seek to capitalize on the window of opportunity any way they can. Depending on the market, sector, or product offer, different businesses will find that their promotional decisions are influenced by these factors. For businesses affected by climate and season, there is often a need to invigorate sales if the weather patterns are unusual or extreme. Selling ski equipment in a poor snow season, for example, can be a major challenge, as can selling swimwear over a rainy summer!

Supplier Relationships and Partnerships

Many businesses source their product ranges from major manufacturers and suppliers. As part of the negotiation process to secure the business of a major client, part of the contracts and terms of trade will often specify the promotional support that is expected from each party. If a product range fails to achieve specified sales targets, is superseded by competitor offers, or approaches the end of its lifecycle, additional contractual pressure may be exerted to force the partner to fund additional promotional activities. In some cases, the vendor and the supplier may agree to engage in cofunded or comanaged sales promotions. Research conducted into sales promotion planning in the New Zealand supermarket industry has revealed that the conflicting goals of these various parties, or inequality in power between the partners might adversely affect the planning process and therefore the campaign outcome (Simpson 2006). After all, in a situation where a business is seeking to boost short-term sales by exerting pressures on a partner to agree to priced-based promotion, but the manufacturer is trying to grow long-term loyalty through brand building, it is unlikely that a ready consensus will be achieved on the best strategy. The research in this case also suggests that as supermarkets have the upper hand in negotiations, their objectives may tend to overshadow those of their partner, so in essence the manufacturer may *lose out* at the negotiating table. These factors, combined with a potential lack of trust in the retailer–manufacturer relationship, and a potential lack of campaign implementation expertise on the part of the retailer, may negatively affect outcomes. Wherever the balance of power rests in a joint promotional venture, involving a partner will to a greater or lesser degree influence the planning process affecting both the nature of the promotion and the subsequent management responsibilities.

Stakeholder Expectations: Contractual, Service, and Legal Obligations

Different business structures present different challenges in terms of the degree to which stakeholder interests are taken into account. A company that owns its own stores and has a good track record in sales promotional management may have little need for external stakeholder involvement in the planning process. For franchise or buying group structures, however, this may not be the case. Franchisees engage with an organization on a formal contract basis. Buying group structures means that the vendors they serve are essentially customers, not employees. The contractual terms, as well as detailing diverse operational provisions and responsibilities, will often determine the level and nature of promotional activity offered by these business structures. If the stakeholder perceives that centralized promotional initiatives are too costly or are not effective, they may challenge the organization's competence and direction, seeking change or challenging intentions. In addition, in almost all countries, sales promotion legislation is highly regulated, with government agencies, consumer advocacy groups, and *watchdog* organizations keeping a close eye on proceedings. If a business has developed a reputation for unethical promotional practices, or has attracted significant criticism from franchisees, vendors, or customers, consideration of these external stakeholder perspectives may be intrinsic to the planning process, especially if litigation, poor publicity, and questionable performance are evident.

Marketing Agency Contribution

Many businesses engage the services of specialist marketing or promotional agencies to assist in the design, planning, and management of their promotions. This is especially the case where promotions have potentially complex legal implications, for competitions, contests, and sweepstakes. Involving an agency at an early or late stage in the planning process will inevitably influence the decision-making process. Agencies can bring new and creative campaign ideas, consumer data, legal and management expertise, and external perspectives to the table. However, an agency is only as good as the brief it receives. Research into businesses and agency relationships has illustrated that organizations may not brief agencies clearly enough on specific objectives and intentions, and this may have a detrimental impact on agency performance and promotional effectiveness (Rhea and Massey 1989). If used effectively, agencies can fulfill a valuable role providing more objective and data-driven insights to support promotional planning decisions. One researcher observed "An agency with no data offering now risks being sidelined in the decision-making process" (Hoffbrand 2007, 11). The decision to use an agency and the skills knowledge and expertise accessed can have a significant effect on the quality of campaign outcomes.

Internal Influences

Market and Brand Position

Businesses adopt a specific market position in relation to their competitors. They also have a unique brand ethos and brand values and target specific consumer demographics to differentiate themselves in the competitive arena. It is important that the marketing, advertising, and promotional strategies adopted are reflective of the market position and brand messaging and are therefore attractive and relevant to core consumer mindsets. Luxury retailers therefore may choose promotional strategies that are nonmonetary and value adding in preference to discounting, which may be used only rarely or at certain times of the year. In this way, they can appeal to more discerning, hedonistic shoppers. This reduces the likelihood of the brand being devalued in the consumers' mind and preserves brand integrity. It also minimizes the chance of downwardly revising reference pricing. Many department stores—historically upmarket entities—have in recent years resorted to more frequent discount activity, as they seek to win back their share of the discretionary spend in the face of competition from both online retailers and fast fashion value retailers like Zara, Topshop, and Uniqlo. Value retailers on the other hand will often introduce a wide range of monetary and value-adding promotions to compete effectively in price-sensitive markets characterized by utilitarian, deal-prone customers.

Marketing Plan Focus and Direction Agenda and Direction

The annual marketing plan developed by the organization will determine the key objectives and strategies that the marketing team will pursue in support of wider business goals. These plans often specify key initiatives in relation to market penetration, sales, customer growth and retention, category and product changes, key sponsorship arrangements, and seasonal events and opportunities. Naturally, the sales promotion strategies and tactics must support this *big picture* marketing plan, so promotional planners refer to the marketing plan as the basis upon which to schedule more specific initiatives and campaigns. This is sometimes conducted simultaneously with marketing planning and sometimes at a later stage, depending on the decision-making process adopted. Sales promotions are also introduced to support the marketing agenda if it is felt an additional lift is required to achieve a specific goal or aim.

Category and Product Sales, Market Share, and Margin Targets

It is important to take into account the detailed financial targets that the organization sets in relation to category, product, growth, and profitability. These targets are monitored and reported regularly and include daily, weekly, monthly period, this year versus last year, year on year growth, and like for like sales analysis against forecast. In order to be responsive to these trends over time, planners must review performance targets, and in consultation with other stakeholders they must propose courses of action that will increase the likelihood of success. There is always a trade-off however. Heavy discounting may boost slowing sales, but it will also negatively impact margins and profitability if not carefully managed. A promotion introduced too early in the season can cannibalize future sales and encourage stockpiling. Ineffective clearance initiatives can leave surplus stock on the shelves making the introduction of new ranges onto the sales floor problematic.

Experience and Preferences of Decision Makers

This is commonly identified as both a positive and negative force on promotional planning. Inexperience on the part of the decision maker, for example, in relation to campaign optimization, data analysis, or negotiating skills may increase the likelihood of poor decision being made. Businesses often make decisions and decide on options and preferences based on their previous experiences. There is a degree of familiarity and certainty in sticking to tried and tested methods, and it is not surprising that those responsible for sales promotions often tend to look back, rather than look forward in the early stages of planning. If a business has favored a particular form of promotion, research conducted in Australia has shown that this can be a strong influencing factor on how much budget is allocated again in the future, revealing "there is a highly significant relationship between retailers' perception of a promotional tool and the budget spent on that tool" (Fam and Merrilees 1996, 338).

When deciding between options, it is worth considering that not all may be considered equally or objectively. Those responsible for planning and budget allocations may be inclined to favor the tried and tested at the expense of the new. Whether these old favorites are in fact the best options is of course debatable. Experience is often a good thing; however, the familiarity that accompanies it can also limit innovation and lead to situations where the same strategies and techniques are used, often long past their sell by date.

Budget Allocation Methods

Sales promotion strategies need funding to bring them to life. The way in which a business allocates funds to sales promotion campaigns will determine the resources available to managers. Sometimes organizations make a broad allocation to marketing, often based on a percentage of sales. This allocation may include funds for marketing advertising and sales promotion, so a degree of negotiation is required on the part of managers to secure an adequate percentage. If sales fall below target in a given year, the available funds may be less than expected, and further negotiations will be required to decide who gets what, and how the available budget will be allocated. In this case, planners ask "how can we best invest the funds available to us?" In other cases, managers may work on detailed, cost-based models that outline the key initiatives considered to be both essential and desirable, which are then presented to internal stakeholders for approval. The dialogue here centers on "these are the resources we need to implement our promotional plans." If cuts to the proposed budget are made, managers must decide on which are the priority initiatives and which must be downscaled or shelved. Sometimes the promotional spend for the previous year is considered and a similar allocation plus a small percentage to cover increased costs is awarded. In other cases, detailed reviews of campaign effectiveness will determine which initiatives are worth pursuing in the future and which underperformed.

Organizational Structure and Internal Stakeholder Dynamics

The internal structure and politics of a business can affect the extent to which internal stakeholders are involved in the promotional planning process. In some cases, responsibility for campaign planning and implementation may lie within a single, siloed department (i.e., marketing). In these cases, the promotional plans will be developed and introduced with minimal consultation. The marketing plan and promotional calendar is developed and refined within the department and subsequently shared with other key departments. These must then organize their forecasting, buying, inventory, distribution, and merchandising activities in support of the various campaigns and initiatives. Other, more informal and progressive business structures and cultures may encourage greater involvement in the early stages of planning. In these cases, there is extensive cross-functional discussion and negotiation. Opinions are sought from peer functions and the marketing and promotional plans evolve over a period of time through a process of negotiation, cooperation, compromise, and sometimes conflict. This can increase the level of understanding and acceptance as the promotional plan is defined by consensus rather than by dictate. There is a risk that in this negotiation process, the decisions and choices that the stakeholders agree on may not in fact be the best decisions, but merely the most familiar, the least risky, or the least contentious. In addition, the opinions and preferences of dominant stakeholders and seasoned managers may take center-stage, but these may not reflect the optimal course of action. This may be especially true when, for example, a new marketing or promotions manager joins a business, but finds that their fresh ideas meet with resistance from the *old school* players even though their proposals may be more progressive.

Campaign Evaluation

Those responsible for sales promotions are often criticized for their lack of rigor in assessing the effectiveness of a campaign against the objectives originally set, failing to apply meaningful measures and metrics. As many promotions involve a significant investment on the part of the business, this is a common bone of contention for the accountants in the organization. Unless campaigns are comprehensively and rigorously evaluated, it is difficult to conduct comparative return on investment analysis to determine which promotions perform best. Similarly, if evaluation measures are only short term in perspective and limited in scope, a clear and comprehensive view of longer-term impact is absent. The degree to which campaigns are objectively evaluated will influence views on their future use. If only limited measures are employed, for example, short-term sales lift, other longer term and potentially negative effects may be overlooked. If a particular form of sales promotion is favored in the business, it is possible that evaluation exercises may be limited and superficial in nature. For those critical of new initiatives, a disproportionate focus on the metrics of a new campaign can also kill off an idea that may be no worse, or in fact better than current alternatives. Finally, in joint venture promotions, the validity of the various partners' performance data may be called into question, especially if the promotion is run on a contractual basis with hard targets and measures specified in the small print. Without a clear basis for evaluation, it is easy for personal preferences and subjective opinions to cloud the understanding of what worked well and what did not. The consensus seems to be however that overall businesses do not do enough to evaluate the efficacy of specific campaign within the promotional calendar. Therefore, the quality of their decision making going forward may be questioned in many cases. In the next chapters, we look at how processes and influences combine in the practitioner's world, to identify opportunities for making better decisions and optimizing the return on promotional investment.

Chapter Highlights

- Key questions need to be answered by decision makers as part of the planning process.
- Sales promotion decisions are made using established processes that may be unique to an organization.
- Decisions will be influenced by a number of internal and external factors.
- Managers need to be aware of the consequences of using ill-defined processes in decision making.
- Some sources of influence may act positively upon the process, while others may have a detrimental, disproportionate, or biased effect.
- There remains a noted disparity between conceptual guidelines and practical approaches.
- A model of decision making with key generic stages can be used to guide the process.

CHAPTER 7

Case Study Research Method

Introduction

It is important to balance both academic and practitioner perspectives when discussing sales promotions management. As well as distilling the findings of a broad field of academic insight, the research conducted for this book involved gaining a tangible insight into how managers in diverse retail and consumer facing organizations made their decisions. This was achieved by interviewing professionals in a variety of organizations, including food retailing, department stores, fashion chains, and automotive accessory retailing. We also sought the opinions of marketing agencies and suppliers involved in sales promotion negotiations. The results of these interviews formed the basis for the case studies presented in subsequent chapters. As valuable research tools, both interviews and case studies need to be carefully structured and applied if they are to be effective in communicating key findings. This chapter explores some of the key principles relating to these research methods, enabling the reader to

- Appreciate the research rigor that was applied to the development of this book
- Understand the principles and processes behind these approaches

This provides a solid basis for understanding the cases presented in subsequent chapters and provides guidance to those wishing to conduct their own research into management decision making.

Research Questions

Central to any research process is the development of clear and focused research questions. For this book, we developed the following list of questions that we wanted to ask.

1. *What are the main decision-making processes used by businesses?*
2. *What factors influence and shape the decision-making process?*
3. *What determines the budget and resource allocations that sales promotions attracts?*
4. *How is the effectiveness of sales promotions gauged?*

We sought to explore the *how and why* of sales promotion decision making to understand the managerial context and identify ways in which managers may make better decisions, presenting our findings in qualitative case study form. Combined with secondary research into decision making, this approach was intended to provide some very detailed insights into contemporary management practice.

Types of Case Study Approach

Three main types of case study have been identified—*explanatory, exploratory, and descriptive* (Yin 2003). The case study approach used for this book encompasses aspects of all three types, as it seeks to *describe* current practice (content analysis), *explore* decision influences (interview), and *explain* decision outcomes (applying models to aid interpretation). Our approach can be alternatively defined as practice orientated, as this form of case study seeks to "describe the design, implementation, and/or evaluation of some intervention, or illustrate the usefulness of a theory or approach to a specific company or situation" (Dul and Hak 2008, 23).

Use of a Semistructured Interview Approach

Due to the nature of the research, we decided that qualitative key contact interviews would form a significant part of the case study data collection. A semistructured interview approach was used, providing flexibility for both interviewees and interviewer for the following reasons:

1. The management environment was not known, nor could be easily predicted. Therefore applying a semistructured interview approach would enable tangents to be investigated and clarification to be sought especially in relation to structure, terminology, and practice.
2. A fully structured interview approach was not deemed appropriate, as variables in context and approach would be investigated.
3. The application of a semistructured interview approach allows relative differences in practices to be explored, and well as reasonable comparisons to be made.

Interview Considerations

In the development of our interview frameworks, it is again necessary to refer to reference sources that illustrate good practice in both question and interview design. These included providing clear briefings, asking focused and brief questions, and avoiding potentially leading questions (Hair et al. 2003). These principles were incorporated within the research process.

Summarizing the Case Study Research Process

One of the keys in gaining credibility for case study research and qualitative studies is to make the case study research procedures and process explicit, so that readers of the study can judge the soundness and appropriateness of the methodology. (Ellram 1996, 114)

It is considered important in any research exercise to apply a rational, structured, and logical approach to data collection. The key process applied by the authors in developing the management case studies contained in this book will now be presented.

Identification of Target Organizations

The research centered on retail and consumer organizations that employed sales promotions as part of their national marketing strategy. The participating organizations had represented a wide range of sectors and ownership models and were therefore considered to be representative of the retail landscape. Industry contacts within the organizations were approached informally to initially discuss potential participation. While this may raise critical questions in relation to objectivity and representativeness, it was considered to be an appropriate approach (i.e., the organizations were not under any obligation, nor were they involved in a direct current client relationship with any of the authors). Once initial informal discussions had taken place, a formal letter was directed to the marketing director in the organization, outlining the research rationale, subject focus, and objectives and seeking formal confirmation of the organization's willingness to participate.

Development of Interviewer's Guide

In order to provide a consistent framework for data collection, it was necessary to develop a detailed interviewer's guide (Ellram 1996). This contains more specific questions relating to each of the major research questions previously presented and will facilitate consistent data gathering across all organizations.

Identification of Key Decision Makers in the Organization

This identification of key contacts was achieved via initial exploratory interviews with senior marketing personnel in each organization. As literature had revealed, different levels of managers have different accountabilities, ranging from the strategic to the operational and tactical. Where possible, the most senior relevant manager in the organization were approached, as well as the managers or agency representatives responsible for campaign design and implementation, in order to provide a balance of perspectives.

Field Research Phase: Data Gathering (Pilot and Main Studies)

Using the research questions developed, evidence was gathered within organizations over two distinct phases: a pilot phase and a main study phase. This evidence was gathered via key contact interviews using the research questions presented previously as the basis for enquiry, supplemented by other information sources gathered in the form of current business documents or archived promotional materials.

Data Analysis

As it is necessary to analyze research findings, interviews were transcribed for analysis. Subsequently, key themes, perspectives, influences, and processes were distilled, providing a solid foundation for case study development and analysis.

Reporting

The key research findings are summarized and reported against the key research questions, with cross-case analysis and management implications being discussed in the final chapter.

Addressing research questions through a case study approach is a valuable research method that enables processes and practices unique to organization to be defined, described, and discussed. It can provide a rich narrative into the realities of organizational practice and for these reasons was selected as the preferred method of investigation.

Chapter Highlights

- A case study approach was adopted as the preferred research method.
- Semistructured interviews were used as the primary source of data collection to answer research questions.
- Each case study has been documented and analyzed and reported in line with best practice principles.

CHAPTER 8

Supermarket Industry

Introduction

This chapter explores promotional decision making in two diverse organizations in the grocery retailing sector. These are a mid-tier independent supermarket group and a major supplier to the group. The chapter provides an overview of the sector and a brief profile of the two main organizations. We map the processes adopted by both businesses and identify the influences that act upon these processes. The chapter also discusses the decision-making agenda, highlighting opportunities for cooperation and potential sources of conflict between the retailer and the supplier of the organizations. This case study provides a detailed insight into how decisions are made and why particular courses of action are pursued.

Industry Overview

The global supermarket industry is one defined by intense competition and continual innovation. Many of the major international chains like Walmart, Tesco, Sainsbury's, and Carrefour have evolved rapidly to meet the demands of the multichannel value-conscious consumer. Advanced distribution systems, online shopping, extensive nonfood product offers, private label expansion, and a resurgence in the popularity of smaller convenience retail formats are testimony to the rapid pace of change in the sector. It is also the sector where sales promotions in all their various forms are used extensively. All major retailers in this field have sophisticated promotional strategies that aim to establish and consolidate their value-credentials as well as leverage in-store purchase opportunities at the point of sale. Discounting and the use of coupons are especially prevalent, as are supplier-funded promotions.

Independent Supermarket Group

This organization is a national grocery retail buying, distribution, and marketing group. It sells national brands and private label ranges in the fresh and ambient categories through a network of company owned and independently operated stores. As a smaller chain, the business is considered to occupy a mid-tier market position with a strong focus on smaller format convenience retailing. The group management supplies products and offers branding, marketing, and promotional support to its network of *members*, depending on their business structure and trading requirements. The specific nature of this business model creates an interesting dynamic for analysis in comparison to more conventional retailer models that own and operate their own network of stores exclusively.

Strategic Marketing and the Sales Promotion Interface

The strategic marketing plan for the group is formalized up to 12 months in advance. Driven by the marketing manager and supported by a small marketing team, the plan is developed taking into account marketing data from previous years. This provides a basis upon which to review future marketing intentions against past performance. Key priorities for this longer-term view include the following:

- Defining the number of new stores required in the network to achieve growth goals.
- Retaining the store base.
- Defining and achieving the sales volumes required from store trading activities.

Effective marketing and promotional activity is central to the key focus on retaining existing stores and growing membership to expand the network of operations.

The general manager summarized the approach taken to marketing planning and its link to promotional agendas:

… we are a pretty informal business from a strategic marketing point of view. There are no committees, there are no councils … we will consult with various people in terms of the broad plan, based on what we've done historically but also based on the overall organizational objectives going forward…. And part of that will also be the marketing plan that supports us actually getting there.

Budgets: A Moving Feast

Budget realities are always top of mind and actual budget allocations are strongly linked to past sales performance. If the group failed to achieve its sales target, for example, it is likely that budgets would need to be revised downward. This would mean compromises would have to be made. The experience and insight of decision makers would determine how these reduced funds would now be allocated to achieve the biggest *bang for the buck*.

Sales Promotion Planning

Planning centers on the development of an annual promotional calendar that details the major campaigns. The calendar is created from the longer-term marketing plan developed by the marketing department. The planning involves close cooperation between the marketing team, buyers, and category managers especially in relation to the timing of new product launches. The proposed calendar is *signed off* by a cross-functional senior management team, although monthly marketing and promotional progress reviews allow tactical flexibility and market responsiveness.

Decision-Making Process

Based on interviews with key personnel in the business and using a simplified model of the sales promotion decision-making model presented in Chapter 6, the key decision stages and notes on their specific nature within the business are presented in Figure 8.1. Under the main process

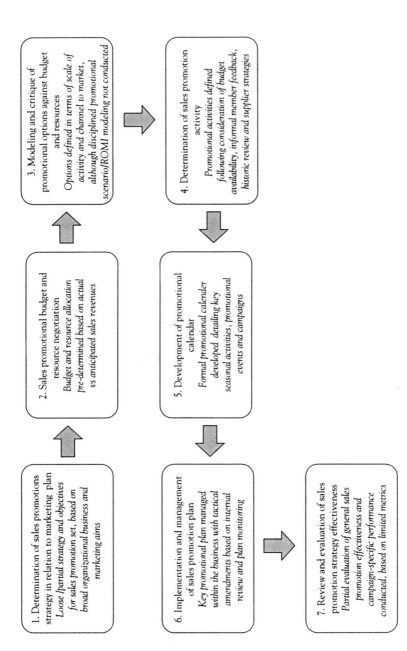

Figure 8.1 Sales promotional decision making in a supermarket group

headings, the approach taken by the group in relation to its promotional decision-making activities is summarized in italics.

Process Observations

Some key insights into the decision-making process are revealed:

1. A clear, workable distinction between marketing and sales promotion activity within the business was not evident, with the boundaries between these distinct activities often blurred. Broad strategic aims for sales and store numbers were identified. However, more specific marketing objectives (relating to brand, customer loyalty, competitive positioning) were not clearly defined. This suggests that promotional activity may be conducted without a clear view of its direct relationship to more specific marketing aims.

2. The objectives set for sales promotions appeared to be often broad or vague. This may in part be due to the fact that the organization, due to its business model, could not comprehensively identify sales across its chain of member retailers at any given time. Stores were not obliged to provide sales data and in addition stores often used different point of sale systems making comparison difficult. As the general manager conceded:

> Because of the lack of data, we've not been able to objectively say we're going to increase our overall store sales by x per cent, 'cause we don't know what the base is. Next year we will.

Further ambiguity was evident when we interviewed the client manager of the marketing agency used by the group to design and manage a promotional competition campaign:

> Client Manager: "Look they wanted to increase participation from previous years. They wanted to get more entries than they got in previous years."

Interviewer: "Did they say how many or by how much?"

Client Manager: "No, they just wanted to do better than they did last year."

3. Budgets for sales promotion activities were determined in advance before campaign planning, based on sales performance. As such, the ability of promotional planners to negotiate internally for funds for new initiatives or to extend existing campaigns was limited. The allocation of funds to specific marketing and promotional purposes was reportedly based on the consideration of two factors: the perceived importance of the initiative and the cost associated with it. As the group placed high importance on the weekly catalogue as a promotional medium, this took precedence in terms of resource allocation, followed by point of sale activity and community engagement.

4. Although consideration of campaign alternatives was reported, the need to satisfy store owners' expectations and preferences in relation to marketing activities could mean that the most popular—if not the most effective—promotional mix could be implemented. As the general manager noted:

Part of that (choosing between promotional options), dare I say it, is the perception of doing something to support the store. So they may see say a monthly ad on television being far more valuable than a major quarterly consumer promotion, because their perception is their brand is on television, their customers are seeing it in their local town, gives them some presence. From their point of view it's perceived as valued. Does it relate back into sales? Well, we don't know.

The group did not appear to have a clear view on the relative effectiveness of different promotional tools. When asked which options were considered most effective, the general manager conceded: "… the honest answer is we don't know. I mean they all contribute to a degree. What the degree is has not been analysed."

5. The group had not comprehensively evaluated the effectiveness of individual sales promotions. Overall promotional performance

was assessed on a simple cost versus revenue calculation and on other broader measures, for example, sales, average basket size, and number of transactions. A key issue that made evaluation difficult was again based on the nature of the business model where, due to independent ownership of stores, point of sale systems were diverse, making data-gathering difficult. As the general manager noted:

> So a lot of it (promotional campaign performance) is certainly not … quantifiable to any great degree; it's anecdotal. But it is the nature of that sort of member-driven business where there's 10 different point-of-sale systems that don't talk to each other … there's just been that lack of information in the business.

Perhaps to counter this, other, more ad hoc evaluation measures were also employed. These included informal feedback gathered from store visits and retailer meetings.

The group sought feedback from its suppliers on how successful they thought particular campaigns had been for their brands and products. However, as the general manager observed, this was not a formalized process:

> Traditionally, again I don't think there's been a formal process for doing that…. So we'll go back and say what did you think? Did you see it on television? What did your reps think in the stores? Was the point of sale put up? Did you see the shelf offer near your products? So we'll try and get that sort of feedback from them … it hasn't been a formal evaluation.

In summary, within the decision-making process identified, there are clear opportunities for improvement. These relate to objective setting, information flow, and campaign evaluation.

Decision Influences

Interviews conducted within the group were analyzed to define the range of influences that shaped the decision-making process (Table 8.1).

Table 8.1 Decision influences

Sales promotion decision influences	
External influence factors	**Internal influence factors**
1. Subjective views and preferences of store owners and operators in relation to sales promotions 2. Competitor activity in the sector can result in tactical amendment to planned promotional schedules 3. Major supplier initiatives (i.e., new product launches) may determine or influence promotional scheduling	1. Historical reliance on the strategic marketing activity calendar as a key determinant of marketing and promotional activity 2. Top line revenue expectations from store networks 3. Lead role of marketing department and merchandise teams in defining the promotional plan 4. Senior management team approval 5. The use of sales promotions as a method of supplier revenue generation 6. Historical budgeting approaches to promotional fund allocation 7. The wish to be seen to *support the store* via numerous promotional initiatives 8. A lack of rigorous campaign evaluation allowing more subjective influence factors to shape promotional decisions 9. The significance of the weekly catalogue as the key promotional medium for the business 10. An emphasis on price and product as key promotional levers 11. The traditional focus around seasonal events to determine promotional activity and scheduling 12. A limited desire to control and coordinate independent supplier promotions

Key Observations

Consideration of the factors that act to shape promotional planning leads to some significant conclusions:

1. There is a strong reliance on previous promotional planning to determine the promotional mix and schedule. This reliance on past history, while offering advantages in terms of risk minimization, may also limit promotional innovation.

2. The group does not collect comprehensive performance data. Lack of accurate information and analysis can lead to subjective decision making. Indeed stakeholder pressure may overshadow fact or logic in campaign decision making.

3. Future promotional budgets are set as a percentage of actual sales revenues. A failure to achieve target sales could result in a reduction in promotional funding. If promotions are central to sales success, a downward spiral of underinvestment may see future sales performance compromised even further.

4. External influences on sales promotion planning appear relatively limited compared to the internal influences identified. The major source of external influence reported is a *leader* group of store owners and operators who, although consulted, are reported to rarely impact or significantly amend the promotional plans set for the business. This may be evidence of a risk-averse culture. The group may therefore present familiar and safe rather than challenging or innovative options to increase the likelihood of acceptance.

Having explored practices in this retail group retail organization, we now consider a supplier's perspective on sales promotion management. Retailer–supplier relationships are an emotive topic in the supermarket industry. Many argue that retailers, due to their power and position, always have the upper hand in negotiations. For competing suppliers keen to secure major customers, dealing with retailers can be a daunting process. Losing a major account can be a severe and sometimes fatal blow. Conversely, retailers often have the luxury of choosing between competing suppliers and products when building their category plans. This has led to allegations of heavy-handed negotiation techniques being employed by retailers to beat suppliers down on price with the threat of de-listing sometimes implicit if suppliers do not agree to accept challenging terms of trade such as high promotional levies, charges, and penalty clauses. When negotiating with retailers therefore, suppliers need to present a robust case not just for their product's integrity and relevance, but also for their expertise in promotional management. Taking this challenging dynamic into account, it is valuable to understand the supplier's perspective, to see how their approaches and views differ from that of a retailer.

Sales Promotions and the Supplier

This company is a leading manufacturer and supplier of branded goods in the beverage category. It supplies major grocery retailers as well as smaller independent chains and outlets with a range of both staple and value-added products.

Strategic marketing planning provides the broad direction and defines the priorities for this supplier. Sales promotions are perceived as fulfilling a key role in keeping brand and product strategies *on track* by influencing sales, responding to competitor activity, and adding value for the consumer. The channel marketing manager explained:

> Tactical promotions ... are borne out of decisions that are made whether they are volume driven, (so we're actually not hitting a number at a particular point in time and sales are actually running low), competitor activity ... for price-pointing, or that we just need to add some value back into that category to drive some growth around what we would normally do .... If you actually get all the elements right of a consumer promotion, you're not only adding value or rewarding loyal people, you're actually ticking the boxes from a volume perspective and also from a gross margin perspective.

Using the example of a recent promotional competition campaign, which offered purchasers of a new range of iced coffee the chance to win a football-themed vacation to Brazil, the channel marketing manager illustrated the importance of sales promotions in encouraging product purchase and trial:

> There is an added value hook to say OK well if I've never actually drunk that I might be enticed enough to actually switch and say that I might try that instead. At the same time I just enter the promotion because I love soccer and I want to go to Brazil.

This campaign generated 124,000 entries, which was considered to be a very successful outcome.

Taking a proactive view on sales promotions can be a negotiating advantage for a supplier in what is a fiercely competitive environment. As well as providing a point of differentiation for the brand or product in negotiations, they can serve as a responsive tool to help both parties manage sales performance more effectively. As the channel marketing manager observed:

> So what they're (the retailer) actually looking for is a point of difference from us as a brand compared to our competitor. Or, if the category actually has had a slight decline and they need a response or an uplift in order to achieve certain sales during that period, then they will come to us and say OK, well what have you got?

There was also consideration given to a campaign's acceptance by the retailer and the impact that it could have on stores and staff, due to its design, especially in relation to additional task requirements. As a brand manager observed, when discussing the choice and design of campaigns:

> It has a lot to do with what has worked before, who the target market is and then also what the retailer is also expected to execute. Say if you had a scratch and win card that the retailer had to hand out with every purchase, that actually has an impact on their employees ... some retailers aren't particularly enthused with that as an option ... others are very keen on having a "winning store" kind of promotion because they view that as unique to them.

The Supplier's Decision-Making Process

Again using our model of decision making, the key stages in the supplier's decision-making approach are presented in Figure 8.2. Under the main process headings, the approach taken by the supplier in relation to its promotional decision-making activities is summarized in italics.

Supplier Process Observations

Some striking differences between the approach taken by the retail group and the supplier are revealed:

1. There is a clear link between the use of sales promotions and the broader marketing and brand agenda. The supplier's marketing teams

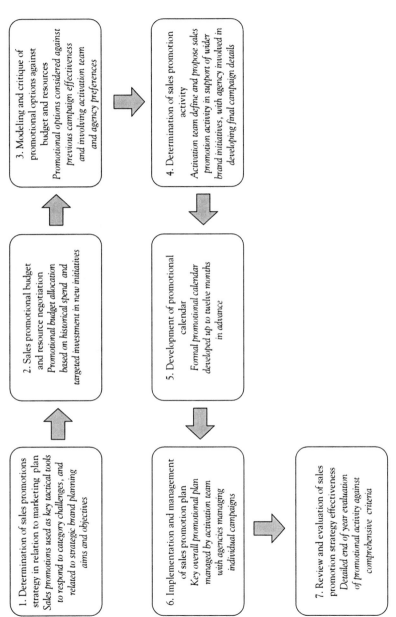

Figure 8.2 Sales promotion decision making for a supplier to the supermarket industry

propose, design, and implement promotional activities to support specific aims and objectives for the brand and the product range. Having a clear, defined view of the aims of a particular campaign was seen as very important as the channel marketing manager emphasized: "So our objectives are very clear with all of our promotions as to what we want to do. It's normally the top two or three objectives that we need to deliver on with any promotional activity."

2. Sales promotional budget allocations are not determined exclusively on the basis of previous spend as new brand initiative demands were considered in budget negotiations. Therefore, the supplier's promotional planning and budgeting activities although influenced by past experiences are not constrained or defined by them. There was also a high emphasis placed on detailed and rigorous historical analysis to shape future decisions:

> So we're actually just about to step into brand planning. So what we did last year ... we're going to revisit and actually do all the analysis ... for every state, every brand, in every category ... We get into what we have put up previously, what actually has worked, can we reinvigorate that, can we actually own that category for a particular period, is it seasonal or not?

3. Sales promotion planning involves a high degree of internal and external negotiation in which many stakeholders are able to influence the decision-making process. This was especially the case of a major retail initiative, such as a new national product launch. Combined with a close working relationship with promotional agencies, this evidences a dynamic and collaborative decision-making process as the channel marketing manager noted that:

> There's a lot of work and effort that goes in behind that, a lot of discussions with (obviously) our customers and also our state sales guys, marketing, manufacturing. Everyone sort of comes together to actually work out what ... that looks like ... so it's nearly a whole business decision when we're actually going to be running a major promotion in a major retailer.

4. Sales promotions are evaluated comprehensively at the end of the financial year. A range of measures are used, including campaign cost, conversion rates, consumer impact, retailer feedback, and sales force feedback. The method of evaluation was formalized via a standard template to ensure consistency in reporting and to make interpretation easier.

Supplier Decision Influences

The key influences on marketing and promotional decision making for the supplier are presented in Table 8.2.

Supplier's Decision-Making Influences: Key Observations

Considering the sources of influence identified, the following observations are presented:

1. Sales promotion decisions are made with the competitive environment clearly in mind. The promotions offered as a consequence are

Table 8.2 Influences on supplier's promotional decision making

Sales promotion decision influences	
External influence factors	**Internal influence factors**
1. Stakeholder (retailer) demands, expectations, and contractual requirements 2. Competitor activity in category and product field areas 3. Consumer buying behavior in response to category or product marketing initiatives 4. Agency views and recommendations in terms of sales promotion function and design	1. Strategic brand aims and objectives 2. Category and product sales, share and margin targets 3. Activation team experience and preference in developing promotional strategies 4. Internal stakeholders involved in the promotional decision-making process, e.g., marketing, manufacturing, and field sales 5. Consideration of impact on store operations of a given promotion 6. Past campaign performance analysis 7. Interpretation of expectations of target consumer 8. An evolving process-driven decision-making approach

therefore market-focused, specific in purpose and consumer focused in nature, as they seek to influence consumer behavior in a challenging environment.

2. As a supplier, there is a clear need to develop initiatives that accommodate client (retailer) expectations of sales and category impact, while at the same time being seen as sympathetic to the operational implications of campaign activation in-store. A planned promotion must have broad acceptance, and must also not be too labor intensive or place too many burdens on store teams. This illustrates the critical interface between supplier organization and retail client in proposing and determining effective sales promotions, and highlights the importance of close communication between these parties as the promotional calendar is developed.

3. The experience of decision makers within the organization is a key asset. However, the extensive use of evaluation data to guide decision making also ensures that the potential for history and cultural preferences to dominate future campaign choice and design will be kept in check.

Chapter Highlights

- The case study provides a review of two main stakeholders in the supermarket industry.
- With the current retailer–supplier market dynamic often reported as pressured, coercive, and price-focused, the knowledge and learning opportunities for both parties may be overlooked.
- Our findings demonstrate that the supplier has a clearer view on purpose, role, design, and evaluation than the retailer.
- In the case of the retailer, difficulties in data gathering were shown to adversely impact the ability to set clear goals and review campaign performance.
- The case studies provide evidence of the potential value in closer retailer–supplier collaboration in campaign design, management, and evaluation.

CHAPTER 9

Hardware and Home Improvement

Introduction

This study focuses on a hardware and home improvement retail group. It reveals how strategic marketing and operational decisions are influenced by diverse stakeholders as part of the process of transforming objectives, aims, and goals into promotional strategies, tactics, and campaigns. The case study reviews a high-profile promotional competition campaign offered by the business. This campaign was chosen as the business saw it as valuable in terms of impact and differentiation. Interviews were conducted with the general manager (operations), the brand manager, and the account manager from the agency who acted on behalf of the organization in marketing and promotional activities. The case study follows the journey from concept to design of this major campaign and reveals some of the complexity involved in translating broad business goals into specific campaign activity in a dynamic competitive environment. In conclusion, the case determines how the effectiveness of this campaign is assessed overall from the perspectives of the major stakeholders involved.

Industry Overview

This sector has experienced a significant boom in recent years. Once the domain of small, local independent retail outlets, the big box evolution has seen major players like Home Depot (United States), B&Q (UK), and Bunnings (Australia) dominate the landscape with extensive product and service offers. The competitive focus for success is on wide ranges, low prices, and compelling promotional incentives. The sector also covers a wide variety of product ranges, home, gardening, outdoor, automotive, and landscaping, for example, for the home improvement enthusiast.

This sector contains a number of different business models. While independent retailers still serve community needs, other models of business organization have evolved to bridge the gap between the big box and the corner store. Franchising or buying group models (where retailers elect to affiliate themselves with an established brand while retaining independence) is commonplace. This case study focuses on promotional decision making in one such organizational structure.

Hardware Buying, Merchandise, and Marketing Group

This group, with a 100 year + heritage, is a distributor of hardware products to a network of several hundred independently owned stores. It also offers supporting services in branding, marketing, and merchandising. In this respect it can be considered to share operational similarities with the food retailing organization discussed previously in the book. With a relatively small head office team, some aspects of marketing and promotional management are outsourced to agencies. This business structure, which shares certain similarities with franchising operations, means that the stakeholder network encompasses both employees (in head office capacities) as well as members who utilize the services of the business while retaining independent ownership and control of their business. The key stakeholders in decision making, referred to in the case, are represented in Figure 9.1.

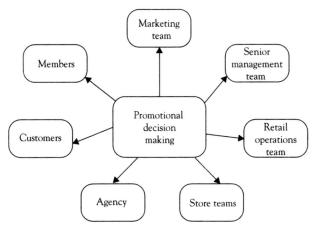

Figure 9.1 Key stakeholders

Management Perspective

The head office team led by the general manager has overall control over marketing and media initiatives. It is responsible for developing and presenting a unified marketing platform that the independent business owners who form the membership base can participate in and benefit from. As the general manager summarized:

> What we do from a head office perspective is pretty much control all the media ... that includes TV catalogues, point of sale ... as an independent franchise group of customers, the franchisees pretty much rely on the brand to pull the consumers into the store, so if there is no marketing department it is questionable as to whether we would have those franchisees as part of our overall business.

Operational Decision Making: Brand Management

The brand manager outlined three overall aims for marketing as a function within the business:

> There's generally three things that we always want to achieve and while it's not a written objective the three things we need to achieve each year by doing the promotional program are: increase sales; increase traffic; grow brand awareness. They're very basic, but generally that's what we work toward.

These three aims, although not quantified, were identified as being the drivers of marketing and promotional activities, forming the basis for the development of the annual marketing plan.

Marketing Plan

Each year the marketing team would work together to develop a marketing *wish list*. This specified all the activities, publications, and promotions that they would like to see implemented in the next 12 months. Budgets and cost projections were modeled against this ideal, identifying the central costs to the organization and the costs to retail store owners in terms of the annual membership levy. The proposed plan and budgets were also a result of the involvement of other key internal stakeholder teams in the decision-making process, namely, the supply chain, retail operations, and merchandise teams. Their contribution influenced the profile of the final marketing proposal, as issues of stock sourcing, availability, ranging, delivery, pricing, and anticipated sales forecasts were considered. This *wish list* was reviewed against revenue projections from retail activity, supplier contribution, and member service fees. In terms of anticipating revenues, and subsequent marketing funds available to drive the process, the brand manager observed:

> We obviously go into the year with an opinion that we're going to get 5, 10 percent increase in sales … the other half of the equation is we also believe we're going to have so many stores as part of this particular group, which will equate to a certain amount of money.

Feedback from Store Owners

The provisional marketing plan was reviewed internally, before being presented to a representative committee of retail store members for feedback and comment. This provided a point of reference and a consultative forum to the organization in matters of marketing and promotional strategy. Any observations or concerns of the committee in relation to the marketing plan, for example, were fed back to the marketing manager and the marketing team for further revision. A similar approach was reported in the overall evaluation of marketing effectiveness, with a stronger emphasis seemingly placed on opinion and perception tan on metrics and measures, as the general manager noted: "It's loosely reviewed in terms of member feedback. They will tell us whether they thought the marketing program was successful or not, from their perspective."

This approach—collaborative and subjective—was evidenced in other areas of decision making including sales promotions.

Sales Promotions in the Business

The group's definition of sales promotions included a wide range of initiatives and mediums, including catalogues, online promotions, trade promotions, and supplier promotions. The key reasons for sales promotions being used by the group were identified by the brand manager as a result of increasing media complexity and fragmentation. Sales promotions were seen as a way of more directly and personally engaging consumers: "Media is getting so fragmented that communicating with more and more people is becoming harder and harder ... doing a sales promotion, we're able to gain people's attention quicker than doing a straight advertising campaign."

Sales Promotional Decision Making

Decision making within the group was characterized by consultation with internal and external stakeholders, as the brand manager observed:

> Marketing will probably instigate the ideas and the wish list ... we wouldn't necessarily take these type of promotions back to merchandise. These promotions would then go maybe to our retail operations team, in relation to them giving us feedback on whether they believe the stores would get on board with it or not in a general sense. And then we would present the overall campaign idea (to the retailer committee).

Once a particular sales promotion had been approved in principle, the brand manager would brief their campaign agency and advertising agency. The agencies would advise on the message, mechanics, channels, and legalities of specific promotional initiatives.

Influences on Choice of Promotion

Return on investment was actively considered in relation to any promotion, as the cost of any promotion was intended to be funded by the revenue it generated. Promotional campaign design involved consideration of the types of consumers that the campaign was intended to attract. For example, the offer of free children's toys for purchases over a specified purchase amount at Christmas time was designed to appeal family shoppers. The simplicity of promotional management at store level was also cited: "It has to be very, very simple in a franchise environment ... if we try to mix it up too much ... the stores physically can't handle the running of that."

Competitor activity and price positioning were also identified as influencing factors in major promotional decisions, especially as the organization was not perceived as the price leader in its market.

Promotional Competition Campaign

A recent promotional competition campaign gave entrants the chance to win $1 million in a chance-based draw. For this major promotion, the main aims were to secure consumer details to develop the marketing database as well as to create a high impact point of marketing differentiation. In addition, the value of providing a point of interest for store owners and staff was also cited, as the brand manager observed: "I think generally the reason why we do competitions is to give them [store owners and staff] something new and fresh and to get them to look at that particular sale in a different light."

Campaign Mechanics

A total budget of $100,000 had been assigned to the campaign. Forty thousand dollars of the $100,000 budget was invested in the development of an insured promotion. The remainder allowed the organization to offer a $500 prize every day of the promotion duration. This was seen as vital to maintaining the stores' focus on reinforcing the promotion. Entry was conditional on making any purchase from any store. Customers were directed to visit a dedicated website to enter. They were also presented with the option to register their entry via SMS. One winner would be chosen at random for the main prize draw. At a special event, they would choose one envelope from 250. One of these would contain the major prize of a check for $100,000. All other envelopes would contain a check for $10,000. The competition was promoted in catalogue advertising, in-store, and through mainstream media advertising. The final profile of the promotion is presented in Table 9.1.

Campaign Design: Process and Influences

The group's two advertising and promotional agencies influenced decisions on whether or not to use promotional competitions as part

Table 9.1 *Campaign profile*

Purchase dependency	Entry platform	Engagement demands	Prize award
Purchase required from any store No minimum purchase value specified	Limited chance based: maximum of five entries per person per day One entry per transaction	Basic contact details required to complete entry online SMS entry requires name and address details	Deferred and staged: one major winner drawn at the end of each month, and one daily minor prize winner announced incrementally

of their creative brief to advice on marketing strategies and tactics. This influence would take into account the aims for the campaign, with the advertising agency advising on *creatives* (themes and messaging) and the promotional agency advising on campaign execution. As the key stated objective of the major competition was to secure customer details, the promotional agency recommended the use of web and SMS entries to avoid the perceived administrative complications caused by recording mail entry details.

Reflecting the nature of consultative decision making in the group's marketing activities, informal feedback from head office staff employees was often sought in relation to campaign design preferences. This feedback could often be quite influential in shaping campaign profiles, as the brand manager observed: " … we pretty much go round the general business and get people's feedback. It's funny, sometimes the option you wanted to go with isn't necessarily the one you end up going with because of that."

Anticipated consumer preference in relation to prizes was also a consideration: "What we try to do is make sure that whatever the promotion is, the prize is actually relevant to the target audience we're trying to communicate with."

In support of this, the group's promotional agency consulted research on the prize preferences of diverse consumer types when advising on design the organization. An additional consideration relating to campaign design centered on the perceptions of the likelihood of winning that customers may hold, especially in relation to the single major prize in the million dollar promotion. As the brand manager explained:

> If consumers think they have high odds of winning, they will be online to enter. So we might have ten products at a thousand dollars, and get two thousand entries, or we might have one hundred at ten dollars and have seven thousand entries.

Other key design and decision influences related to geography and the cost of prize distribution. The brand manager highlighted:

> One thing that's important when we do competitions is fulfilment, so how are we going to get those prizes to those winners? ... We've got stores all over ... and potentially if we do a barbeque giveaway ... that barbecue worth a 1,000 bucks might cost us a 1,000 bucks (to deliver).

Perceived Benefits of the Promotion

The key benefits cited for the decision to use this form of campaign are related to cost effectiveness, differentiation, member engagement and consumer interest, an increase in sales activity, and the potential to drive footfall and increase brand awareness. As the business was price competitive in its market, but not a clear price leader, promotional competitions were also seen as a way of exercising a degree of control and influence within stores and over product: "It's kind of like a silent sales person ... it helps us direct a consumer in a store we don't own to buy a product we want to try and control."

Having considered the group's view on this form of campaign, it is important to explore the role and contribution of the agency that is tasked with designing the competition against their client's brief.

Agency Perspective

The group employed the services of a specialist marketing agency to advise on matters of campaign design, theme, messaging, and activation.

A campaign brief was prepared by the group's marketing team to form the basis for campaign design. The agency account manager reported that although certain element factors were specified in the brief, there was scope for creative contributions from the agency in terms of message, mechanics, and implementation. The process that defined the creative exchange between the groups and its agency is represented in Figure 9.2.

Within this process, the agency had consulted the group in relation to the use of the insured draw mechanism. The group was, however, focused on the idea offering a major *headline* prize (as opposed to a larger number of smaller main prizes) and therefore held firm views on the nature of the dictated prize profile. The account manager reflected: "They (the group) are very involved, they wanted big money ... they wanted to communicate a million."

It was acknowledged by the agency manager that there was little science behind the group's decision to want to offer this particular prize. She did, however, acknowledge that using consumer research data allowed the agency to offer suggestions and alternatives in relation to prize choice, based on the reported popularity of certain kinds of rewards: "As to the decision making we'll encourage them to lean a certain way and we'll come up with the prizes ... and put forward recommendations."

The account manager considered the campaign to have been highly successful, based on the number of entries received. However, it was evident that the agency was to a degree unaware of the total investment, or the expectations of their client in relation to return on investment: "That worked really well ... but I don't know their (the organisation's) full investment, so the return on investment ... I'm not too sure, but from our perspective it was a successful promotion judged on the number of entries."

This sentiment was echoed by the general manager on a separate occasion, when considering the impact of the campaign on sales: "The million dollar entry gave us a lot of entries, but didn't necessarily give us a massive sales increase."

In this case, the campaign could be perceived as successful against its key aim of contributing to the customer database. However, despite the requirement to purchase as a condition of entry, the campaign did not have a major impact on sales. It is worth considering if the design

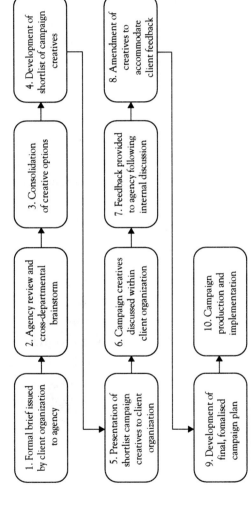

Figure 9.2 The campaign decision-making process between group and agency

of the campaign (where no minimum purchase amount was specified to facilitate entry) could have been better structured to grow both sales and database registrations. This raises questions in relation to the synergy between campaign aims and campaign design, especially where either firm budgets or entrenched preferences are evident. Using the example of the group's input into the design of another promotional competition, the influence exerted by the group's decision makers was seen as a compromising factor. The budget-related rationale for the short duration (19 days) of the promotion was considered to have been a major factor in the poor results achieved. As the account manager observed:

> They wanted weekly prizes, and couldn't afford it ... it's always money, and unfortunately you get what you pay for. It was a very low budget and everything we had presented they had scaled down—the promotional period, the weekly prizes ... so instead of increasing their budget or changing the prizes, they said "so we can afford nineteen of them, let's do it for nineteen days."

This decision was seen to have compromised campaign impact and yield, for example, as the period recommended by the agency for promotional competition duration was four to six weeks, compared to the 19 days that the promotion was actually run.

Measuring Campaign Effectiveness

Agency

The key measures used by the agency were identified as the number of entries and participation trends, for example, the spread of entries over the campaign lifecycle. Whether sales data was included in their evaluation exercise depended on whether their clients shared sales data with agency. The consumer's preferences in relation to campaign popularity had not been formally sought in recent times. As the account manager conceded: "Years ago we used to. We don't now ... we used to ask questions more about the brand, not about the mechanics and what made them buy."

Group's View

Evaluating these forms of campaigns, and assessing the return on investment for such campaigns was considered still to be an evolving skill in the retail business. This was due in part to unclear responsibilities in relation to campaign management. As the brand manager conceded: "We had different people managing competitions previously, and there wasn't really any structure ... if the members weren't angry about it we'd do it again."

Conclusion

This case presents an insight into sales promotion management in relation to a specific form of campaign. As evidenced, the organization has good intentions in relation to the use of this specific form of promotion. It seeks to differentiate itself in the marketplace, provide a captivating and compelling offer to its consumers and provide retailers within the group with an exciting headline campaign to drive store visitation and sales. However, ambiguity is noted in relation to the establishment of clear objectives, the choice of campaign profile and subsequent evaluation, even with the services of a professional promotional agency at its disposal. It can be argued that in this case greater goal clarity, objectivity in campaign decision making, discipline in evaluation, and a higher degree of receptiveness to agency intelligence could help to facilitate a stronger return on marketing investment.

Chapter Highlights

- Sales promotions are seen as valuable to communicate with and engage consumers in *noisy* media environments.
- Stakeholder inputs in this case play a significant role in the development and refinement of marketing and promotions strategies.
- Promotional competitions can be used for a variety of purposes including building awareness, growing databases, and increasing sales.

- Clear objectives need to be established for these campaigns to make sure they are fully leveraged.
- Information sharing between client and agency is essential if comprehensive evaluation of campaign effectiveness is to be carried out.

CHAPTER 10

Department Store

Introduction

This chapter focuses on sales promotion decision making in a department store chain. The case study explores the thinking *behind the scenes* shared by decision makers in this business. The relationship between marketing strategy and promotion planning is determined with the key drivers behind these activities being discussed. The process adopted within the marketing team is presented and a significant range of internal influence factors that act upon this process are identified.

Industry Overview

The department store sector has come under enormous pressure recently from both the expansion in online retailing (in mass and niche segments) and through the growth in *fast-fashion* retailing evidenced by the global success of Zara, Top Shop, H&M, and ASOS. In a highly competitive and evolving sector, department stores perhaps more than any other retail format face challenges of relevance, value, promotional appeal, and customer connection.

Department Store Business

The organization operates a chain of department stores. The stores offer a range of product categories, including fashion, cosmetics, home electronics, children wear, white goods, and furniture. It operates at a mid to upper position in the market, competing with other chains as well as with mid-market and discount players.

Strategic Marketing Planning

The annual marketing plan produced by the business is influenced by longer-term goals and objectives. These are detailed in the retailer's long five-year plan. Key influences in relation to strategic marketing planning, which facilitated sales promotion campaign planning were identified as the tangible resources (budget allocations) available and the experience of decision makers in shaping promotional agendas. This experience was valued particularly due to the timing of budget allocations. Marketing planning commenced in December, before finalized budgets were confirmed in March. This demanded a degree of flexibility and responsiveness in the initial planning stages when final budgets were uncertain. Reference to the previous year's marketing plan was identified as the starting point for future marketing planning, with key calendar dates and events providing the framework for the next year's activity planning. The general manager expressed reservations in relation to an over-reliance on history: "I'm also really conscious that if you always look backwards then it's very hard to come up with new idea."

In a fiercely competitive environment, a major focus for the marketing team was to ensure high visibility in relevant media channels. As the general manager observed: "I want to go where the eyeballs are. That's actually a bigger statement than it sounds because that is saying there is a shift in the media landscape and we need to plan for that shift in landscape."

To facilitate this high visibility, the marketing department needed a strong relationship with the merchandise department, with whom they collaboratively determined the specifics of the marketing agenda for the forthcoming year. The general manager saw the marketing department's role as central in ensuring that the cornerstones of the retail brand strategy are reflected in the marketing activities. This was, as he said, "to ensure that whatever ends up going out the door has a certain robustness to it compared to what the company strategy is."

This emphasis on flexibility, responsiveness, and relevance was also noted in sales promotion planning exercises.

Sales Promotions

The business engages in a wide range of promotional activity, including discounting, major seasonal sales, product bundling, loyalty-program member exclusive offers, and promotional competitions, for example.

Supplier promotions within the stores are also fairly commonplace. In these cases, campaigns are initiated, designed, and managed by the supplier and approved by the category manager. Marketing department involvement in supplier-led promotion cases is limited to the consideration of visual merchandising compliance and branding consistency postapproval. Nonmonetary supplier led promotions were seen to as a way to boost lackluster sales without resorting to costly markdowns. Using the example of a promotion that offers customers of a cookware range, the chance to win sporting event tickets the general manger reflected:

> If you're going to think in the most simplistic way about how our merchants work here—right or wrong—they're looking at the X range and they don't think it's working then they will go to (the supplier) and say let's invigorate this product by marking it down and you guys pay for the cost of the markdown. Whereas (the supplier) will look at it from the complete flipside which would be yep, I want to invigorate this range but I don't want to mark it down because it devalues the brand and I don't want to pay your markdown. I'm getting these (event) tickets for free so I'm more than happy to advertise off my own bat.

In contrast to this supplier-driven approach, for major calendar promotions linked to seasons, brands, and categories, marketing, merchandising, PR, and event teams would be involved in the proposal, design, and management of these internally driven major campaigns.

Sales promotion plans were driven by seasonality, as key promotions were structured around the fashion calendar. The merchandising team determined which brands and products would be sold each season and was involved with the marketing team in defining the key promotional periods, themes, and messages. The marketing department produced the formal promotional calendar, which was refined as a result of internal consultation with key product category executives and store representatives. All attention was on driving sales, as the marketing manager observed: "Everything that we do is to promote to actually encourage a sales component and drive sales, otherwise it's not getting the return on investment that we require."

Sales Promotion Decision Making: A Flexible Approach

Decision-making systems and methods were described by the marketing manager as highly consultative and flexible in nature. This allowed the marketing plan to be amended according to dynamic trading conditions, as well as enabling the business to capitalize on promotional opportunities that were presented. In one example, a car manufacturer wanted to hold a promotion for its product range within a number of retail stores. It was considered that the customers of the department store would be an attractive demographic to target. The campaign was further supported by a paid advertisement in the department store's magazine. Clearly, advertising revenues were a major driver of the decision to host this promotion, although the advertising manager admitted there were no hard and fast criteria against which the planned promotion would be assessed:

> It's not something that we planned ... How this came about was (the supplier) approached us because they were keen to get their cars in-store, and that's how this opportunity arose ... There wasn't really a criteria as such. It was whether the stores were open to it, so an email goes out to the stores just saying whether they would be open to doing this within the store, whether they had the space in the store, whether we could get the cars into the store ... and no there wasn't ... not really ... any real reason as to why we would do it, I suppose.

Competitor activity was also identified as a significant influencing factor that brought about the need for flexibility:

> You can't put your head in the sand and ignore what your competitors are doing. An example is a competitor's gone out and done a particular promotion on something ... you might not necessarily match it, but you want the price perception or the value component so you might do something to ensure that you're not being out-gunned in that particular component.

As part of the promotional planning process clear sales objectives was set for specific promotional activities, based on past performance: "They all have sales dollars they need to achieve, which will be plus or minus ... on last year, to achieve the overall sales dollar."

In deciding between promotional alternatives, the marketing manager reported that there was a degree of brainstorming and discussion as options were considered. There was however no formal, documented process or method for evaluating the relative merits of competing options, nor to evaluate relative return on marketing investment (ROMI) potential: "We definitely have a decision process ... Whether it's written down? Probably not."

The final determination of promotional activity and the consolidation of the promotional calendar was described as a collaborative and fluid process, refined through weekly cross-functional meetings and progress reporting. Sales promotion activity was evaluated in weekly meetings and acted as a source of reference for future campaigns: "I guess decisions are made and documented on what particular elements worked and did not work, that you can either take forward in the coming weeks or use again, the same time round next year."

Final sales promotion activity is determined as a result of regular stakeholder dialogue, based on the initial marketing and promotion plans developed by the marketing department and subsequent tactical amendments. The general manager noted that the annual promotional planning process commenced in January, in preparation for the start of the new financial year. This resulted in the production of a defined and detailed marketing and promotional calendar, the progress and impact of which is regularly reviewed. Regular consideration of sales performance and return on investment was identified as central to the assessment of sales promotion and marketing effectiveness, which was conducted weekly and quarterly. The broad impact of promotional activity on consumers was also assessed as part of quarterly research commissioned by the organization, although this was defined as over-arching research, which included assessing the effectiveness of media campaigns on consumer awareness, but did not report specifically on individual promotional campaigns.

Decision-Making Process

The sales process decision-making process used within the business is summarized in Figure 10.1.

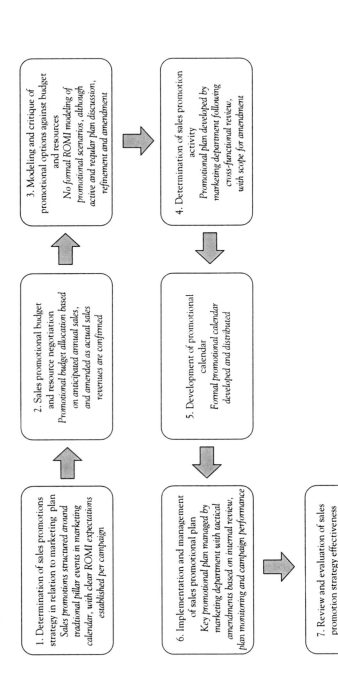

Figure 10.1 Sales promotion decision making in a department store business

Process Observations

Considering the approach taken in the business, and the rationale offered for the specific approach, the following insights into the process are that

1. Clear performance expectations are established in relation to specific major sales promotion initiatives, in terms of contribution to sales and ROMI with promotions focusing on key *pillar* events in the marketing year.

2. The budget allocation process for sales promotion activity reflects the need for flexibility and tactical amendment, as sales promotion planning must in this case be commenced prior to actual budgets being established.

3. The modeling and critique of promotional options is a more informal and organic process, relying on history, experience, judgment, cross-functional interaction, and campaign review. This approach to promotional planning could result in a familiar and acceptable (but not necessarily optimal) promotional plan.

4. The organization reports a strong incidence of regular campaign monitoring and sales promotion plan review, the results of which facilitate tactical plan amendment to ensure that sales promotions continue to be responsive to changing market conditions, new product and category variables, and competitor activity.

Decision Influences

The key influences on sales promotion decision making are summarized in Table 10.1

Influence Observations

Considering these factors, it is proposed that:

1. The competitive dynamics in this brand-driven, discretionary retail sector mean that both brand alignment and the ability to respond tactically to changing circumstances are paramount for decision makers. Those with responsibility for sales promotions need therefore to

Table 10.1 Sales promotion decision influences

External influence factors	Internal influence factors
1. Seasonality in relation to key fashion seasons and key fashion calendar events 2. Competitor activity 3. Trading environment and the impact on sales revenues generated against forecast 4. Key supplier stakeholders 5. Media and creative agency contribution to promotional messaging	1. Brand proposition 2. Wider marketing agenda and direction 3. Sales targets within the business set against specific promotional activity 4. Actual versus anticipated sales determine resource availability 5. Internal stakeholders (merchants, marketing, stores) 6. Organic and flexible nature of decision making in relation to sales promotions 7. Review of previous campaign success 8. Broad research on consumer sentiment in relation to promotional activity 9. Desire to develop positive consumer sentiment in relation to promotional activity 10. Historic promotional event platforms usage (i.e., traditional stocktake sale and mid-season sales) 11. Marketing department perspective on and proposal of projected promotional structure 12. Known or projected product events (i.e., new product or range launches) 13. Function of promotions as potential revenue generators via partner contribution or sponsorship

be agile and flexible in their approach, yet also remain conscious of the longer-term brand strengths and priorities.

2. Collaborative relationships between the marketing, merchandise, and retail store teams are considered essential to facilitate this brand-centric agility. Decisions involving multiple internal stakeholders will often have brand, category, inventory, and margin implications; therefore, regular communication and consultation is essential to ensure that marketing plans and sales promotion responses remain in sync.

3. Consideration of return on promotional investment is identified as a strong internal decision influence. This was reported to be largely based on comparing the performance of current campaigns to

previous ones, as opposed to utilizing best practice or benchmark reference data. This could potentially compromise promotional ROMI spend if previous campaigns were not fully optimized. Using historical performance in order to gauge recent campaign effectiveness may provide a basis for comparison. It may however limit more rigorous assessment of campaign impact and the subsequent consideration of alternatives.

4. Suppliers could, as illustrated, influence the promotional landscape in the business. It is interesting to note that supplier promotions were not centrally controlled, scheduled, or coordinated, but were often a result of buyer–supplier negotiations. Due to the high number of supplier promotions evident at any one time, the collective activities of suppliers could impact consumer perceptions, creating a confusing promotional landscape in some categories. Hence, while the individual influence a supplier can exert by bringing a *good idea to the table*, the collective impact may be less positive for the brand overall.

Chapter Highlights

- Department stores operate in a highly competitive and constantly evolving mature retail sector.
- As a result, the business places high emphasis on maintaining a targeted promotional presence using relevant channels.
- Strong internal relationships are seen as central in ensuring that effective promotional campaigns are delivered that support brand strategy.
- Maintaining flexibility and responsiveness is vital to combat competitor activity.

CHAPTER 11

Cross-Case Analysis

Introduction

The three cases presented represent different market sectors, ownership models, and supply chain positions. The first case discussed the perspectives both of a grocery retail organization and a supplier to the industry. The second case took a close look at the processes and influences that relate to a specific form of campaign in the hardware and home improvement sector. The third focused on a department store chain. Although the ways in which decisions are made within each of these businesses differ, shaped by both sector and market-specific forces, it is valuable to consider the overall insights and learnings that these very different cases can collectively reveal. This chapter identifies and discusses some of the *common ground* in strategic marketing and promotional decision making that we observed across the cases. This analysis paves the way for the conclusions and recommendations for practitioner improvement presented in the final chapter.

Marketing Decision Making

In all cases, a link between marketing strategy, marketing plans, and sales promotion activity was evidenced. Sometimes however, short-term targets, rather than long-term business ambitions and intentions, seemed to take precedence. This challenges the conventional wisdom that long-term strategic aims and objectives should form the basis for short-term actions and initiatives, that is, sales promotions. Only in the case of the department store was tangible reference to a five-year plan for the business cited. It is worth questioning therefore to what extent diverse organizations specifically define and determine their longer-term ambition in relation to sales, branding, market share, and consumer engagement. Strategic marketing intentions need to be clearly defined so that promotional planners can develop sustainable and relevant promotions. Otherwise, they may work hard to develop specific campaigns that are based on vague or poorly communicated goals and aims. This reveals the importance for promotional planners to look *upstream* to the more strategic aims of the organization when developing their campaign plans, and having a clear picture in mind at all times of the evolving nature of the business they are seeking to support, at least to the best extent they can.

In the case of the retail organizations (more so than in the supplier case), discussion of strategic marketing quickly led to the discussion of functional marketing and promotional planning. This illustrates a conceptual difficulty in some cases in differentiating long-term marketing strategy from short-term promotional tactics. The distinctions between marketing, advertising, and promotion often become blurred in practice. This lack of clarity can have negative consequences for the decision-making process.

The cases support for the view that marketing decision making is a consultative venture (Webster 2005). In all instances, proposals for marketing activities were open to influence and negotiation from other business functions. In many cases, this consultative approach was actively pursued rather than reluctantly accommodated. Although the organizations adhered to culturally distinct procedures (involving history, stakeholder consultation, judgment, data evaluation, etc.), they did not appear to apply an objective, tangible model or a strong theoretical basis to guide their decisions. In essence, all the approaches appeared to be *home grown*. This supports the view of experts in the field that managers often rely on localized and qualitative knowledge and judgment to shape their decisions, rather than relying on tested models or constructs (Ardley 2005; Little 2004; Low and Mohr 1999). The evidence endorses the view that a model-based approach may have too many limitations to be of practical use (Ardley 2005; Chakravarti, Mitchell, and Staelin 1981; Davies 1993; Low and Mohr 1999). For those working in marketing, or consulting with a range of organizations at a strategic level, finding a solid conceptual basis for understanding *the way we do things around here* may remain elusive. The cases of the hardware retail organization and the independent supermarket group make an interesting contribution to the discussion of marketing management approaches. This is because these organizations have less control over the marketing mix and promotional offers presented to consumers. They do not dictate what individual stores stock or sell nor control the localized marketing activities. Therefore, a mix of central and local promotional activity is evident. Company-owned, company-operated business models have a clearer *line of sight* in relation to their promotional intentions and are able to dictate and implement centralized marketing plans. This raises the question of the degree of influence that stakeholder both internal and external exert within the process.

Sales Promotion Planning

History, culture, and experience have been identified as significant factors that influence promotional planning in the three cases presented. This supports the view that perception and preference are significant factors in promotional decision making (Fam and Merrilees 1996). This often intuitive approach will not guarantee that the promotional mix is optimized. Some promotional tools and tactics were given preference based on a perception of their contribution without an appropriate level of critical rigor. This does not mean however that these perceptions and preferences should not be challenged, neither should their continued value and contribution be assumed in a rapidly evolving business context. Our research revealed that promotional alternatives were not consistently evaluated by either objective return on marketing investment (ROMI) analysis modeling or the critical comparison of campaign alternatives, supporting the calls for more coherent systems of planning (Simpson 2006).

Stakeholders

In all cases, complex, unique stakeholder involvements and diverse consultative networks and points of reference were identified, which influenced the ways in which the organizations developed their marketing strategies and plans. These distinct and sometimes organic processes provide support for claims that where exactly marketing decision-making responsibilities lie is poorly understood (Harris and Ogbonna 2003). This *stakeholder-centric* approach may serve to *keep the customers happy,* especially in franchise or buying group structures. Stakeholder influence, unless carefully managed, however, could compromise objective and optimal decision making. Consensus may not always be the best course of action. Stakeholders often have strong opinions, but may not necessarily possess adequate understanding of marketing and promotional issues to make an informed decision.

Sales Promotion Budget Allocation

There was strong evidence in the cases of both past budget allocations and projected sales forecasts determining available resources to fund future sales promotion activity. This would suggest that objective-based sales promotion budgeting has yet to gain functional acceptance with decision makers, who still appear to look back and look forward but do not fully capitalize on the opportunity to evolve promotion planning with a *clean sheet* approach.

Agency Briefings

There is evidence in at least two of the case studies that the campaign briefs given to marketing and promotional agencies by the businesses were very broad. The supermarket group, for example, did not communicate a tangible sales target to its agency. There was also evidence that potentially vital sales information that could have helped the agency to conduct pre- and postevaluations to determine campaign ROMI was not shared by the hardware organization. Clear and comprehensive briefings have been identified as a critical factor in ensuring promotional effectiveness (Rhea and Massey 1989). In both these cases, however, this appears to have been lacking, compromising the ability of the respective agencies to fully define the needs of the businesses and to comprehensively gauge campaign effectiveness.

Evaluating Promotions

Our cross-case analysis reveals a strong reliance on the use of sales data to assess marketing effectiveness in the short term, with much less emphasis on longer-term multifactor marketing impact assessment. It is interesting to consider whether this focus has in fact led to an increase in business dependency on promotions. As the businesses relied largely on short-term sales-related measures to determine marketing impact, the contribution of longer-term advertising and brand-building activities may be over-looked. Our analysis therefore supports the view that the increase in the proportion of marketing budgets allocated to short-term promotions may lie in the use of short-term measures to review overall marketing impact (Stewart and Gallen 1998). This approach has received criticism (Ziliani 2006) as it does not facilitate the holistic assessment of long-term mar-keting impact. Hence, longer-term strategies (e.g., those that are loyalty based, brand centered, or targeted toward customer franchise building [CFB]) may not yield an immediate, measurable benefit within a limited timescale, but they can still be very effective.

Commentators have criticized what they perceive as a less than rig-orous approach to the evaluation of sales promotions against specific objectives (Ziliani 2006). This is largely substantiated in our cross-case analysis as it revealed that the evaluation of sales promotions was not consistently or comprehensively conducted (with the exception of the supplier to the grocery industry). In addition, in the majority of cases no clear, measurable objectives for sales promotions were identified. These findings support the view that the relationship between sales promotions and profitability may not be understood by businesses (Srinivasan and Anderson 1998).

Conclusion

This chapter has analyzed some of the major issues and limitations relating to sales promotion decision making. Overall, many of the major concerns expressed by expert commentators appear to have a strong basis in truth. Sales promotions are enormously significant, vital, and prevalent in the consumer environment. However, our cross-case study provides tangible insights into where process improvements could be made. As highlighted earlier in this book, sales promotions are a contentious area in marketing. Common criticisms are leveled at marketers for setting vague campaign objectives, their failure to fully consider options and alternatives when defining the final mix, and their preference for monetary rather than non-monetary promotions. These factors, combined with a lack of coherent models and frameworks and an often superficial or short-term approach to evaluation, may be the reason why so many sales promotions are perceived to underperform. The final chapter will offer guidance as to how the sales promotion planning process can be leveraged to improve both the performance and the perceptions of this diverse body of campaign options.

Chapter Highlights

- Short-term targets and measures often take priority over longer-term aims and goals.
- The approaches taken to sales promotion planning do not benefit from a firm conceptual basis.
- Decision-making approaches may be consultative but not optimal.
- Campaign alternatives are not critically evaluated due to the influence of history and preference.
- Evaluation measures may lack rigor and have a short-term focus.
- Agencies may not receive comprehensive briefings from their clients limiting their ability to interpret needs and report on campaign impact.

CHAPTER 12

Improving Sales Promotion Decision Making

Introduction

In this final chapter, we bring together the model of sales promotion decision making, the case studies, and the subsequent analysis of these cases. This forms the basis for our recommendations to industry practitioners on how more effective sales promotions decisions can be achieved. These evidence-based recommendations, we assert, will ensure that promotional planning approaches deliver maximum value and return on investment for the business and its stakeholders.

Sales Promotions Revisited

As highlighted in earlier chapters, sales promotions are an important marketing activity for both consumer-focused organizations and their suppliers. The investment cost is often considerable and the impact that campaigns have on brand perception, customer experience, sales, and profit are very significant. As has been revealed, the effectiveness of sales promotions can often be compromised by a combination of:

- Unclear objectives
- A highly consultative approach to campaign design and management
- An overreliance on history and preference in the choice of campaign offer
- A short-term approach to evaluation

Taking into account the research insights presented and the case analysis conducted in Chapter 11, we now present our recommendations to managers engaged in sales promotion planning. We believe that these recommendations, if adopted, will improve decision outcomes and help to ensure that sales promotions are better designed, better targeted, more effective, and more profitable.

In order to structure these recommendations, the model of sales promotion decision making presented in Chapter 6 will be used as the basis for discussion, to provide clear guidance to managers at each stage of the decision-making process. The model is shown in Figure 12.1.

The research presented in this book has revealed that the decisions often have many sources of influence and can be often procedural and organic—rather than conceptual or objective in nature. Many researchers have challenged the degree to which decisions are likely to be optimized through this approach and have questioned to what degree objectivity may be sidelined in favor of judgment and preference. For practitioners, it is vital to consider the balance of subjectivity and objectivity within the planning processes. It is recommended that a robust model or framework such as the one presented is used by managers in their planning activities.

Recommendation 1: Establish Clear Sales Promotion Aims and Objectives That Are Tangibly Linked to Wider Marketing Strategies

It is essential to ensure that sales promotional strategies are aligned with (and supportive of) wider brand value and marketing positioning. The reference points for any sales promotion planning activity should be the longer-term business goals and the marketing strategy. Planners must be aware of what the business is trying to achieve in terms of these wider goals and aims before considering specific courses of action. Knowing the major aims and initiatives provides a solid foundation that will ensure that sales promotions—although tactical and short term in nature—are synergistic with headline calendar events and complimentary to business ambitions. If, for example, the business is aiming to reposition itself in the marketplace, the types of sales promotion campaigns that are employed may have to evolve to reflect this intention, with the promotional mix changing over time to include a higher proportion of nonmonetary promotions. This may help to change the perceptions of the business as a price-based, discount operator in the customers' eyes.

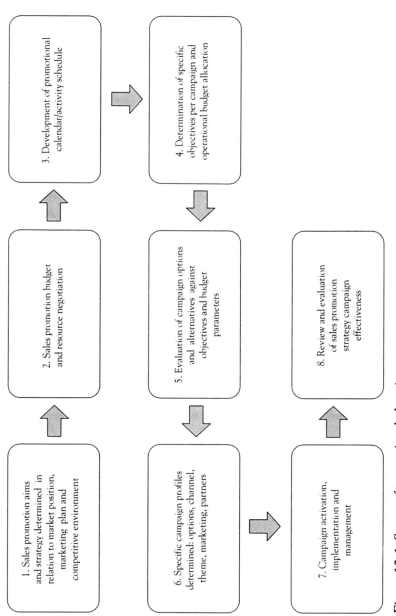

Figure 12.1 Stages of promotional planning

Internal Communications

It is also important for sales promotion management to have a clearly defined rationale and strategy that identifies and communicates the robust relationship between business aims and promotional agendas. This will communicate to the business that there is a strong and relevant foundation for promotional activity and there is a clear purpose, paradigm, and perspective that governs planning activities.

At this *top line* planning stage, it is important to consider key calendar events that are significant for the business and for particular categories and products. This will involve discussions with members of the marketing team, buyers, and category managers to identify what their priorities are, as well as establish timelines for new range introductions, key seasonal events, supplier dynamics (i.e., new product launches), and sponsorship initiatives, for example.

Recommendation 2: Negotiate on Needs, Not on History

The research revealed that often sales promotion budgets were determined by reference to past spend or allocated as a proportion of sales. This approach is problematic for two reasons:

1. It does not accommodate emerging channels that may require additional start-up funding in comparison to previous year's budget allocation.
2. It can mean that in times of sales decline, less money is allocated to sales promotions. If the sales decline is due to stronger competitor activity, or is a result of the impact of a new market entrant, this may be detrimental to future recovery and set promotional responsiveness on a downward spiral.

Detailed budgets should be constructed that cost the campaigns, which are anticipated for the forthcoming year individually and collectively. This will communicate what the *ideal* draft promotional plan will look like and determine the required investment necessary to implement and execute. Clear costings based on concise objectives and planning provides a strong foundation for resource negotiation and increases the chances of budget demands being realized. This is a much more successful negotiating strategy than discussing budget demands in terms of *last year +/– 5 percent* and shows the negotiator to be strategic, well organized, authoritative, and in control. It is a good idea to approach suppliers to gauge their willingness to fund or support planned campaign over the forthcoming year. This option should be kept in reserve in case of a budget deficit.

Recommendation 3: Develop a Clear Plan of Attack

Following negotiations on budgeting and resources, planners will have a clear idea of the funds available and can focus their attention on specific planning activities leading to the development of a firm promotional calendar. Promotional planners need to invest significant time and energy mapping promotional activity over the course of a year. This involves scheduling specific campaigns and initiatives that are supportive both of the marketing agenda and the competitive realities. Promotional planning should also accommodate the insights from previous discussions with category managers, buyers, and suppliers to ensure that every opportunity is leveraged. This should be approached with an open mind regardless of the previous year's activity. This will also ensure that supply chain and inventory considerations can be accommodated to ensure adequate stock holdings at key times. Customers often complain that they were attracted to a retail store by a compelling promotion, only to find that the featured product was out of stock.

It is important to ensure that promotional *bottlenecks* are avoided. Often there is simply too much promotional activity going on at any one time, which can cause confusion for shoppers as well as creating excessive workloads for store-based staff. Promotional plans should therefore balance both promotional activity across the board as well as within specific departments and categories to avoid *promotion fatigue.*

Finally, sales promotion professionals need to allow a degree of flexibility and responsiveness in the planning process to enable tactical response to competitor or market-related issues. This may involve putting key suppliers on alert that promotional support may be required, subject to market conditions.

Recommendation 4: Establish Clear Campaign Objectives

It is essential that each campaign has clear objectives that determine and communicate role, function, and performance expectations. As the research has revealed, all too often sales promotions have vague objectives, or sometimes none at all. Due to the significant investment costs associated with campaign management, it is vital that all stakeholders have a clear view of:

- Why the promotion is to be offered
- What it will aim to achieve
- How success can be measured

Without this clear vision, it is easy to lose sight of goals and purpose and it can be difficult to communicate campaign rationale to internal and external stakeholders. It also makes comprehensive evaluation problematic and can cause dissent and tension between stakeholders who may be confused about just why the campaign was offered and how effective it was. If outside agencies are used, it is imperative that they receive a clear and formally documented briefing. This will mean your campaign aims will not be *second guessed* and the performance of the campaign partner can be ascertained. If no clear rationale for offering a specific campaign can be identified, then consider why the campaign is being proposed in the first place.

Recommendation 5: Consider All Options

As illustrated in Chapters 4 and 5, there is a wide range of options, both monetary and nonmonetary, available to decision makers. All three cases revealed that history, preference, and stakeholder influences played a leading role in campaign choice and design. We recommend that managers widen their thinking and deepen their knowledge base to proactively and comprehensively consider and evaluate all campaign design options in relation to clearly stated objectives. There is a vast body of research relating to sales promotion choice and efficacy waiting to be capitalized upon for those who wish to develop their professional competence. Managers are encouraged to take the initiative in accessing this body of knowledge as well as forge partnerships and relationships with experts in the field on a mentorship or consultative basis.

In addition there are numerous seminars, workshops, and conferences at which practitioners can grow knowledge and share expertise. There are also professional associations for marketing and sales promotion professionals through which learnings are often shared.

If a new campaign option is identified or proposed, of which the business has no prior experience, it is important to keep an open mind. A marketing agency may, for example, be asked for evidence of prior campaign success. This will provide planners with a knowledge base to assist in their decisions. Alternatively, an initial test or pilot campaign may give an early read on suitability and effectiveness prior to a major rollout.

New technologies and emerging channels can also mean that an option previously considered inappropriate, too costly, or too labor intensive may have gained new traction and popular acceptance. What is certain is that not exploring or experimenting and doing the *same old—same old* means that history will be repeated at the expense of innovation and entrepreneurship. Ultimately, competitive advantage will be compromised.

Recommendation 6: Better by Design

Having determined the specific promotional mix, it is time to get creative. Sales promotions work better if they have an innovative theme and a powerful message. This is where the accountants leave the room and the marketing creatives get to work. Whether a mid-season sale, a loyalty-program-based retailer-customized promotion or a promotional competition, campaigns need to be both inspirational and accessible. A discount can be positioned either as a clearance event or as an opportunity to purchase early for Christmas, for example. A buy one get one free (BOGOF) offer can be marketed as a subtle value-add in the case of cosmetics, or as a high profile not-to-be missed deal as in the case of fast food. This is a good opportunity for planners to once again consider the alignment between marketing strategy and promotional theming. It is unlikely, for example, that Rolex or Louis Vuitton would ever offer a *mega-deal*. Often, if promotional design expertise is limited within the business, the services of an external agency can be used to develop campaign themes, messages, and motivations.

Recommendation 7: Plan to Succeed

It is important to ensure that the planning and implementation of campaigns goes smoothly. This means ensuring adequate and timely communication with all stakeholder parties, including marketing, buying, category managers, store managers, store staff, suppliers, and agencies. All too often in retail, stories abound of a huge bundle of promotional materials turning up at the loading dock, heralding an imminent campaign of which the team had no prior knowledge, with not enough resources on hand to ensure timely activation.

It is important to ensure that there are sufficient resources within the head office team to deal with questions and queries, from stores and customers, as well as deal with the administrative implications of campaign participation. This may mean bringing in extra support to process rebates in a timely fashion or designing a process to enable promotional competition entry campaigns to be verified or judged.

It is also important to determine the channels through which the promotion will be presented and capitalized upon. Some consideration may have been given to this at earlier stages in the planning and costing process, but this is the time to consolidate that thinking. If a social media site needs to be designed and established, for example, enough notice needs to be given to enable this to happen. If a promotional competition is offered, permits will need to be applied for leaving enough time for authorization to be granted. If webpages need to be updated, then once again sufficient notice needs to be given, taking into account timelines and workloads.

For major campaigns, it is also good to get feedback from target customers on design, appeal, and access. Establishing a focus group of core customers to facilitate this can be very cost effective to ensure that campaigns are on track and on message.

Recommendation 8: Evaluate, Learn, Re-evaluate

With clear campaign objectives established, the foundations are in place for a thorough campaign evaluation. Using these objectives as a point of reference enables a clear assessment to be made of the impact and effectiveness of the campaign:

- Were sales and profit targets achieved?
- Was surplus inventory reduced?
- Did market share grow?
- Was the new product launch successful?

Some measures of effectiveness will be purely financial and sales related, while others may be more diverse in nature. These may involve, for example:

- Monitoring customer awareness of a new product; and
- Measuring the degree to which customer engagement and learning had grown as a result of campaign participation.

Long-Term Measures

It is essential also to consider not just short-term measures, but also longer-term indicators. Research has revealed strong evidence that short-term sales-related data is used as a key point of reference. There is less evidence of longer-term evaluation across a broader and more comprehensive range of marketing-related measurements. There are some significant long-term implications of promotional activity to consider:

- Did shoppers remain loyal to the new brand that was heavily promoted or did they switch back at the end of the campaign?
- Were future sales cannibalized as a result of shoppers stockpiling?
- Did overall category sales grow as a result of product-specific promotions?
- Which campaign did customers recall after the event?
- Which had the greatest lasting appeal?
- Did the business grow short-term sales, but at the expense of longer-term margin averages?

By having a clear and holistic view of campaign effectiveness, businesses can make insightful decisions on campaign effectiveness, and re-evaluate options for future campaign planning. Due to the significant investments attributed to sales promotions and the high profile they enjoy, the importance of this cannot be underestimated.

Conclusion

As highlighted, sales promotions are a major business activity, commanding significant resources. Sharing the stage with marketing and advertising, sales promotions help to drive sales, cement competitive advantage, and engage consumers. Despite their prevalence, sales promotions and management approaches to promotional decision making remain under-researched. As has been revealed, sales promotions are often criticized for failing to achieve the targets set for them. Those who share responsibility for promotional planning may also find themselves justifying their approaches and defending their actions, competing for scarce resources with other business units.

This book serves as a valuable resource for managers seeking to improve their effectiveness in this field. By presenting detailed research findings that center on management approaches, campaign options, and industry practice, the reader has gained an essential understanding of the role, function, and benefits of sales promotions. In addition, the model of decision making and the core recommendations provide the tools to enable managers to be more effective in their day-to-day activities. The case studies provide industry-specific insights that furnish the reader with the realities of professional practice to enable them to better critique their own—or their clients' or other stakeholders'—approaches.

The benefits of sales promotions for retailers, suppliers, manufacturers, and customers have been detailed. By using the knowledge and information contained in this book, we are confident that these benefits can be more effectively and consistently realized. Thank you for reading!

Chapter Highlights

- It is important to establish a clear link between sales promotion planning and wider business goals.
- Negotiate budgets based on projected needs not solely on past activities.

- Develop a clear promotional calendar to establish the *big picture* for sales promotions in the forthcoming year.
- Develop clear objectives for each campaign.
- Actively consider all promotional alternatives and develop a knowledge base in relation to campaign choice and effectiveness.
- Invest time and energy focusing on the creative messaging of campaigns to ensure relevance and attractiveness for target consumers.
- Plan to succeed by considering the operational implications of campaign activation.
- Evaluate both short- and long-term measures of campaign effectiveness thoroughly and consistently.

References

Ailawadi, K.L., and S.A. Neslin. 1998. "The Effect of Promotion on Consumption: Buying More and Consuming It Faster." *Journal of Marketing Research* 35, no. 3, pp. 390–8.

Ardley, B. 2005. "Marketing Managers and Their Life World: Explorations in Strategic Planning Using the Phenomenological Interview." *Marketing Review* 5, no. 2, pp. 111–27.

Argo, J.J., and K.J. Main. 2008. "Stigma by Association in Coupon Redemption: Looking Cheap because of Others." *Journal of Consumer Research* 35, no. 4, pp. 559–72.

Ashworth, L., P.R. Darke, and M. Schaller. 2005. "No One Wants to Look Cheap: Trade-Offs Between Social Disincentives and the Economic and Psychological Incentives to Redeem Coupons." *Journal of Consumer Psychology* 15, no. 4, pp. 295–306.

Ataman, M.B., H.J. van Heerde, and C.F. Mela. 2010. "The Long-term Effect of Marketing Strategy on Brand Sales." *Journal of Marketing Research* 47, no. 5, pp. 866–82.

Baker, R. 2011. "Energizer Puts Brake on Sales Offers 'that Trash Brand Value'." *Marketing Week* (01419285) 34, no. 37, p. 5.

Barat, S., and L. Ye. 2012. "Effects of Coupons on Consumer Purchase Behavior: A Meta-Analysis." *Journal of Marketing Development and Competitiveness* 6, no. 5, pp. 131–44.

Bell, D., and C. Hilber. 2006. "An Empirical Test of the Theory of Sales: Do Household Storage Constraints Affect Consumer and Store Behavior?" *Quantitative Marketing and Economics* 4, no. 2, pp. 87–117.

Bell, D.R., G. Iyer, and V. Padmanabhan. 2002. "Price Competition Under Stockpiling and Flexible Consumption." *Journal of Marketing Research* 39, no. 3, pp. 292–303.

Blattberg, R.C., R. Briesch, and E.J. Fox. 1995. "How Promotions Work." *Marketing Science* 14, no. 3, pp. G122.

Bodily, S.E., and R.A. Mohammed. 2006. "I Can't Get No Satisfaction: How Bundling and Multi-Part Pricing Can Satisfy Consumers and Suppliers." *Electronic Commerce Research* 6, no. 2, pp. 187–200.

Bruce, N., P. Desai, and R. Staelin. 2006. "Enabling the Willing: Consumer Rebates for Durable Goods." *Marketing Science* 25, no. 4, pp. 350–66.

Cadman, E. 2014. "UK Retail Sales Fall as Discounts Curb Food Price Inflation." http://www.ft.com/intl/cms/s/0/11808c08-a842-11e3-a946-00144feab7de .html#axzz31ZTLBBGW (accessed November 20, 2014).

Chakravarti, D., A. Mitchell, and R. Staelin. 1981. "Judgment Based Marketing Decision Models: Problems and Possible Solutions." *Journal of Marketing* 45, no. 4, pp. 13–23.

Chen, H., H. Marmorstein, M. Tsiros, and A.R. Rao. 2012. "When More Is Less: The Impact of Base Value Neglect on Consumer Preferences for Bonus Packs over Price Discounts." *Journal of Marketing* 76, no. 4, pp. 64–77.

Chiambaretto, P., and H. Dumez. 2012. "The Role of Bundling in Firms' Marketing Strategies: A Synthesis." *Recherche et Applications en Marketing* (English Edition) (AFM c/o ESCP-EAP) 27, no. 2, pp. 91–105.

Choi, B.J., J. Kissan, and J. Lemieux. 2010. "Time-Inconsistent Preferences vs. Price Discrimination: How do Firms Increase Profits via Mail-in Rebate Promotions?" *Advances in Consumer Research* 37, pp. 504–5.

Chung, H.-L., Y.-S. Lin, and J.-L. Hu. 2013. "Bundling Strategy and Product Differentiation." *Journal of Economics* 108, no. 3, pp. 207–29.

Cook, W.A., and V.S. Talluri. 2004. "How the Pursuit of ROMI Is Changing Marketing Management." *Journal of Advertising Research* 44, no. 3, pp. 244–54.

Cooper, L. 2011. "Promotions Switch Focus to Added Value." *Marketing Week* (01419285) 34, no. 26, pp. 27–30.

Corkindale, D. 2009. "Are Marketers Only Half Right?" *Marketing Review* 9, no. 1, pp. 19–29.

Coulter, K.S., and A.L. Roggeveen. 2014. "Price Number Relationships and Deal Processing Fluency: The Effects of Approximation Sequences and Number Multiples." *Journal of Marketing Research* 51, no. 1, pp. 69–82.

Cowell, D.W. 1984. "Sales Promotions and the Marketing of Local Government Recreation and Leisure Services." *European Journal of Marketing* 18, no. 2, pp. 114–20.

Davies, M.A.P. 1993. "Using the AHP in Marketing Decision-making." *Journal of Marketing Management* 10, no. 1–3, pp. 57–73.

de Pechpeyrou, P., and P. Odou. 2012. "Consumer Skepticism and Promotion Effectiveness." *Recherche et Applications en Marketing* (English Edition) (AFM c/o ESCP-EAP) 27, no. 2, pp. 45–69.

DelVecchio, D., H.S. Krishnan, and D.C. Smith. 2007. "Cents or Percent? The Effects of Promotion Framing on Price Expectations and Choice." *Journal of Marketing* 71, no. 3, pp. 158–70.

Demirag, O.C., O. Baysar, P. Keskinocak, and J.L. Swann. 2010. "The Effects of Customer Rebates and Retailer Incentives on a Manufacturer's Profits and Sales." *Naval Research Logistics* 57, no. 1, pp. 88–108.

Dhebar, A., S.A. Neslin, and J.A. Quelch. 1987. "Developing Models for Planning Retailer Sales Promotions: An Application to Automobile Dealerships." *Journal of Retailing* 63, no. 4, p. 333.

Dibb, S. 2002. "Marketing Planning Best Practice." *Marketing Review* 2, no. 4, pp. 441–59.

Dickinger, A., and M. Kleijnen. 2008. "Coupons Going Wireless: Determinants of Consumer Intentions to Redeem Mobile Coupons." *Journal of Interactive Marketing* 22, no. 3, pp. 23–39.

Ducoffe, R.H., and E. Curlo. 2000. "Advertising Value and Advertising Processing." *Journal of Marketing Communications* 6, no. 4, pp. 247–62.

Dul, J., and T. Hak. 2008. *Case Study Methodology in Business Research.* Oxford, UK: Butterworth-Heinemann.

Eaton, B. 2013. "The Necessity of Driving Sales." *Cabinet Maker* no. 5840, p. 34.

Effective Sales Promotion: Playing to Win over the Customer. 2014. Pitney Bowes Australia Pty Ltd.

Ehrenberg, A.S.C., K. Hammond, and G.J. Goodhardt. 1994. "The After-Effects of Price-Related Consumer Promotions." *Journal of Advertising Research* 34, no. 4, pp. 11–21.

Ellram, L.M. 1996. "The Use of the Case Study Study Method in Logistics Research." *Journal of Business Logistics* 17, no. 2, pp. 93–138.

Erutku, C. 2006. "Rebates as Incentives to Exclusivity." *Canadian Journal of Economics* 39, no. 2, pp. 477–92.

Fam, K.S., and B. Merrilees. 1996. "A Promotion Mix Budgeting Model for Retailing." *International Review of Retail, Distribution and Consumer Research* 6, no. 4, pp. 373–94.

Fibich, G., A. Gavious, and O. Lowengart. 2007. "Optimal Price Promotion in the Presence of Asymmetric Reference-Price Effects." *Managerial and Decision Economics* 28, no. 6, pp. 569–77.

Fogel, S.O.C., and C.G. Thornton. 2008. "What a Hassle! Consumer Perceptions of Costs Associated with Sales Promotions." *Journal of Promotion Management* 14, no. 1–2, pp. 31–44.

Franklin, P. 2001. "Problems and Prospects for Practice and Theory in Strategic Marketing Management." *Marketing Review* 1, no. 3, pp. 341–6.

Gaidis, W., and J. Cross. 1987. "Behavior Modification as a Framework for Sales Promotion Management." *Journal of Consumer Marketing* 4, no. 2, p. 65.

Gao, F., O.C. Demirag, and F.Y. Chen. 2012. "Early Sales of Seasonal Products with Weather-Conditional Rebates." *Production and Operations Management* 21, no. 4, pp. 778–94.

Gardner, M.P., and R.A. Strang. 1984. "Consumer Response to Promotions: Some New Perspectives." *Advances in Consumer Research* 11, no. 1, pp. 420–5.

Gardener, E., and M. Trivedi. 1998. "A Communication Framework to Evaluate Sales Promotion Strategies." *Journal of Advertising Research* 38, no. 3, pp. 67–71.

Geurreiro, R., A. Santos, J.A. SilveiraGisbrecht, and B.S. Ong. 2004. "Cost Implications of Bonus Pack Promotions Versus Price Discounts." *American Business Review* 22, no. 2, pp. 72–81.

Gow, G. 2007. "The Right Tools." *Marketing Management* 16, no. 3, pp. 32–36.

Hair, J.F., Jr., and B. Babin, A.H. Money, and P. Samouel. 2003. *Essentials of Business Research Methods.* New York: John Wiley and Sons.

Harris, J. 1997. "The Effects of Promotional Bundling on Consumers' Evaluations of Product Quality and Risk of Purchase." *Advances in Consumer Research* 24, no. 1, pp. 168–72.

Harris, L.C., and E. Ogbonna. 2003. "The Organization of Marketing: A Study of Decentralized, Devolved and Dispersed Marketing Activity." *Journal of Management Studies* 40, no. 2, pp. 483–512.

Hartley, S.W., and J. Cross. 1988. "How Sales Promotion Can Work for and Against You." *Journal of Consumer Marketing* 5, no. 3, pp. 35.

Haskins, J.B., and W.C. Hugli, Jr. 1969. "Evaluating the Effects of Company Promotional Activities: A Neglected Area for Research and Management Attention." *Journal of Marketing* 33, no. 4, pp. 66–68.

Heiman, A., B. McWilliams, Z. Shen, and D. Zilberman. 2001. "Learning and Forgetting: Modeling Optimal Product Sampling over Time." *Management Science* 47, no. 4, pp. 532–46.

Helgesen, T. 1992. "The Rationality of Advertising Decisions: Conceptual Issues and Some Empirical Findings from a Norwegian Study." *Journal of Advertising Research* 32, no. 6, pp. 22–30.

Henderson, T., and N. Arora. 2010. "Linking a Social Cause to Product Promotions: Why it Works and How to Make it More Effective." *GfK-Marketing Intelligence Review* 2, no. 1, pp. 9–15.

Hill, J., and S.K. Harmon. 2007. "Male Gender Role Beliefs, Coupon Use and Bargain Hunting." *Academy of Marketing Studies Journal* 11, no. 2, pp. 107–21.

Hill, C.J., and S.K. Harmon. 2009. "Attitudes Toward Coupon Use and Bargain Hunting: An Examination of Differences by Gender." *Academy of Marketing Studies Journal* 13, no. 1, pp. 67–78.

Hoffbrand, J. 2007. "Are Agencies Up to the Customer Insight Challenge?" *Precision Marketing* 19, no. 12, p. 11.

Hu, N., L. Liu, I. Bose, and J. Shen. 2010. "Does Sampling Influence Customers in Online Retailing of Digital Music?" *Information Systems and e-Business Management* 8, no. 4, pp. 357–77.

Jedidi, K., C.F. Mela, and S. Gupta. 1999. "Managing Advertising and Promotion for Long-Run Profitability." *Marketing Science* 18, no. 1, pp. 1–22.

Jobber, D. 1973. "Evaluating the Effectiveness of Below-the-line Promotion: A Critique." *European Journal of Marketing* 7, no. 1, pp. 64–69.

Johannes, A. 2008. "Playing the Game." *Promo* 21, no. 10, p. 26.

Jude, G., and C. Singh. 2012. Telstra's Report: How Mobility is Changing the Rhythm of Australian Retail. http://www.telstra.com.au/business-enterprise/download/document/business-enterprise-teg1398_mobility_retail_white_pages_v08_hr_singles.pdf

Kim, H. 2013. "How Variety-Seeking Versus Inertial Tendency Influences the Effectiveness of Immediate Versus Delayed Promotions." *Journal of Marketing Research* 50, no. 3, pp. 416–26.

Kimball, R. 1989. "An Exploratory Report of Sales Promotion Management." *Journal of Consumer Marketing* 6, no. 3, p. 65.

Knight, E. 2012. "Discounting is the New Retail Reality." *The Sydney Morning Herald*, February 1. http://www.smh.com.au/business/discounting-is-the-new-retail-reality-20120131-1qrh0.html (accessed May 13, 2014).

Knight, S. 2013. "Australian Store Implements $5 Cover Charge to Combat Showrooming." http://www.techspot.com/news/52088-australian-store-implements-5-cover-charge-to-combat-showrooming.html (accessed July 5, 2014).

Kondo, F.N., and M. Nakahara. 2007. "Differences in Customers' Responsiveness to Mobile Direct Mail Coupon Promotions." *International Journal of Mobile Marketing* 2, no. 2, pp. 68–74.

Kopalle, P.K., C.F. Mela, and L. Marsh. 1999. "The Dynamic Effect of Discounting on Sales: Empirical Analysis and Normative Pricing Implications." *Marketing Science* 18, no. 3, pp. 317–32.

Kotler, P. 2009. "Sales Promotion: Kotler on Marketing." http://www.marsdd.com/mars-library/sales-promotion-kotler-on-marketing/ (accessed September 5, 2014).

Laran, J., and M. Tsiros. 2013. "An Investigation of the Effectiveness of Uncertainty in Marketing Promotions Involving Free Gifts." *Journal of Marketing* 77, no. 2, pp. 112–23.

Lee, Y.-J., and Y. Tan. 2013. "Effects of Different Types of Free Trials and Ratings in Sampling of Consumer Software: An Empirical Study." *Journal of Management Information Systems* 30, no. 3, pp. 213–46.

Lenskold, J. 2007. "Unlock Profit Potential." *Marketing Management* 16, no. 3, pp. 26–31.

Liao, S.-L. 2006. "The Effects of Nonmonetary Sales Promotions on Consumer Preferences: The Contingent Role of Product Category." *Journal of American Academy of Business, Cambridge* 8, no. 2, pp. 196–203.

Little, J.D.C. 2004. "Models and Managers: The Concept of a Decision Calculus." *Management Science* 50, pp. 1841–53.

Liu, T.-C., T. Cheng, and F.-Y. Ni. 2011. "How Consumers Respond to the Behavior of Missing a Free Gift Promotion: Inaction Inertia Effect on Products Offered as Free Gifts." *Journal of Social Psychology* 151, no. 3, pp. 361–81.

Low, G.S., and J.J. Mohr. 1999. "Setting Advertising and Promotion Budgets in Multi-Brand Companies." *Journal of Advertising Research* 39, no. 1, pp. 67–78.

Lowe, B., and B.R. Barnes. 2012. "Consumer Perceptions of Monetary and Nonmonetary Introductory Promotions for New Products." *Journal of Marketing Management* 28, no. 5–6, pp. 629–51.

Macé, S. and S.A. Neslin. 2004. "The Determinants of Pre- and Postpromotion Dips in Sales of Frequently Purchased Goods." *Journal of Marketing Research* 41, no. 3, pp. 339–50.

Marcotte, P. 1989. "Charity Sweepstakes Under Fire." *ABA Journal* 75, no. 4, pp. 24.

Marshall, J. 2007. "Are Finance and Marketing Getting Closer?" *Financial Executive* 23, no. 2, pp. 46–48.

Marshall, R., and W. Na. 2000. "How Much is Enough? A Preliminary Empirical Study of the Price Tolerance Zone in Singapore." *Advances in Consumer Research* 27, no. 1, pp. 30–33.

Mazumdar, T., S.P. Raj, and I. Sinha. 2005. "Reference Price Research: Review and Propositions." *Journal of Marketing* 69, no. 4, pp. 84–102.

Mohammed, R. 2010. "Art of Discounting." *Sales & Service Excellence* 10, no. 11, p. 12.

Mondroski, M.M., L.N. Reid, and J.T. Russell. 1983. "Agency Creative Decision Making: A Decision Systems Analysis." *Current Issues & Research in Advertising* 6, no. 1, pp. 57–69.

Neff, J. 2011. "Why Promotion May End Up a Bad Deal for Packaged Goods." http://adage.com/article/news/promotion-end-a-bad-deal-packaged-goods/148569/ (accessed May 12, 2014).

Nijs, V.R., M.G. Dekimpe, J.B.E. Steenkamps, and D.M. Hanssens. 2001. "The Category-Demand Effects of Price Promotions." *Marketing Science* 20, no. 1, pp. 1–22.

Olsen, M.G., and M. Halliwell. 2007. "Intangible Value: Delineating Between Shades of Gray." *Journal of Accountancy* 203, no. 5, pp. 66–72.

Ong, B.S. 2008. "The Impact of Consumer Perceptions of, and Attitudes Toward Mail-in Rebates on Effectiveness of Rebates." *Journal of Promotion Management* 14, no. 1–2, pp. 45–58.

Palazon, M., and E. Delgado-Ballester. 2009. "Effectiveness of Price Discounts and Premium Promotions." *Psychology & Marketing* 26, no. 12, pp. 1108–29.

Palazón-Vidal, M., and E. Delgado-Ballester. 2009. "Effectiveness of Price Discounts and Premium Promotions." *Psychology & Marketing* 26, no. 12, pp. 1108–29.

Panzone, L., and R. Tiffin. 2012. "The Impact of Price Promotions on Producer Strategies in Markets With Large Product Heterogeneity." *Agribusiness* 28, no. 4, pp. 421–39.

Peattie, S. 2003. "Applying Sales Promotion Competitions to Nonprofit Contexts." *International Journal of Nonprofit and Voluntary Sector Marketing* 8, no. 4, pp. 349–62.

Peattie, K., and S. Peattie. 1995. "Study of Sales Promotion Competitions." *European Journal of Marketing* 29, no. 5, pp. 16.

Peattie, K., S. Peattie, and E.B. Emafo. 1997. "Promotional Competitions as a Strategic Marketing Weapon." *Journal of Marketing Management* 13, no. 8, pp. 777–89.

Pechmann, C., and T. Silk. 2013. "Policy and Research Related to Consumer Rebates: A Comprehensive Review." *Journal of Public Policy & Marketing* 32, no. 2, pp. 255–70.

Penning, A. 2013. "Sample Packaging Engagement." *Global Cosmetic Industry* 181, no. 3, pp. 46–48.

Percy, L., and R. Elliott. 2005. *Strategic Advertising Management.* 2nd ed. Oxford, UK: Oxford University Press.

Permut, S.E. 1977. "How European Managers Set Advertising Budgets." *Journal of Advertising Research* 17, no. 5, pp. 75–79.

Peterson, R.T. 1969. "Experimental Analysis of Theory of Promotion at Point of Consumption." *Journal of Marketing Research* 6, no. 3, pp. 347–50.

Picconi, M.J., and C.L. Olson. 1978. "Advertising Decision Rules in a Multibrand Environment: Optimal Control Theory and Evidence." *Journal of Marketing Research* 15, no. 1, pp. 82–92.

Qiang, L., and S. Moorthy. 2007. "Coupons Versus Rebates." *Marketing Science* 26, no. 1, pp. 67–82.

Quelch, J.A., and K.E. Jocz. 2010. "Government Adoption of Sales Promotions: An Initial Appraisal." *Journal of Public Policy & Marketing* 29, no. 2, pp. 189–203.

Raghubir, P. 2004. "Free Gift with Purchase: Promoting or Discounting the Brand?" *Journal of Consumer Psychology* 14, no. 1–2, pp. 181–6.

Raghubir, P., J.J. Inman, and H. Grande. 2004. "The Three Faces of Consumer Promotions." *California Management Review* 46, no. 4, pp. 23–42.

Rajagopal. 2008. "Point-of-Sales Promotions and Buying Stimulation in Retail Stores." *Journal of Database Marketing & Customer Strategy Management* 15, no. 4, pp. 249–66.

Rao, V.G. 2009. "Effect of Sales Promotions on Consumer Preferences—The Moderating Role of Price Perceptions and Deal Proneness (A Study of FMCG Products)." *Vilakshan: The XIMB Journal of Management* 6, no. 1, pp. 1–18.

Rhea, M.J., and T.K. Massey Jr. 1989. "Contrasting Views of Effectiveness in Sales-Promotion Relationships." *Journal of Advertising Research* 29, no. 5, pp. 49–56.

Richards, T.J. 2007. "A Nested Logit Model of Strategic Promotion." *Quantitative Marketing and Economics* 5, no. 1, pp. 63–91.

Riggans, V. 2012. "Price Promotions." *FMCG* 18, no. 7, pp. 16–18.

Sarin, S., T. Sego, and N. Chanvarasuth. 2003. "Strategic Use of Bundling for Reducing Consumers' Perceived Risk Associated with the Purchase of New High-Tech Products." *Journal of Marketing Theory and Practice* 11, no. 3, pp. 71–83.

Schlereth, C., C. Barrot, B. Skiera, and C. Takac. 2013. "Optimal Product-Sampling Strategies in Social Networks: How Many and Whom to Target?" *International Journal of Electronic Commerce* 18, no. 1, pp. 45–72.

Schultz, D.E., B. Cole, and S. Bailey. 2004. "Implementing the 'Connect The Dots' Approach to Marketing Communication." *International Journal of Advertising* 23, no. 4, pp. 455–77.

See, E. 2006. "Bridging the Finance-Marketing Divide." *Financial Executive* 23, no. 6, pp. 50–53.

Sherwood, T. 2006. "Effective Sampling Strengthens Brands." *Global Cosmetic Industry* 174, no. 9, pp. 32–34.

Shibin, S., A.M. Parker, and K. Nakamoto. 2007. "The Effects of Price Discount and Product Complementarity on Consumer Evaluations of Bundle Components." *Journal of Marketing Theory and Practice* 15, no. 1, pp. 53–64.

Shu-Ling, L. 2006. "The Effects of Nonmonetary Sales Promotions on Consumer Preferences: The Contingent Role of Product Category." *Journal of American Academy of Business* 8, no. 2, pp. 196–203.

Silva-Risso, J.M., R.E. Bucklin, and D.C. Morrison. 1999. "A Decision Support System for Planning Manufacturers' Sales Promotion Calendars." *Marketing Science* 18, no. 3, p. 274.

Simester, D. 1997. "Note. Optimal Promotion Strategies: A Demand-Sided Characterization." *Management Science* 43, no. 2, pp. 251–6.

Simonson, I., Z. Carmon, and S. O'Curry. 1994. "Experimental Evidence on the Negative Effect of Product Features and Sales Promotions on Brand Choice." *Marketing Science* 13, no. 1, pp. 23–40.

Simpson, L.S. 2006. "Enhancing Food Promotion in the Supermarket Industry: A Framework for Sales Promotion Success." *International Journal of Advertising* 25, no. 2, pp. 223–45.

Sinha, P.K., and P.V.R. Prasad. 2004. "Reference Price: Impact of Shopper's Behaviour at the Store." *Decision* (0304-0941) 31, no. 1, pp. 19–50.

Solcansky, M., and I. Simberova. 2010. "Measurement of Marketing Effectiveness." *Economics & Management*, pp. 755–9.

Soman, D., and J.T. Gourville. 2001. "Transaction Decoupling: How Price Bundling Affects the Decision to Consume." *Journal of Marketing Research* 38, no. 1, pp. 30–44.

Spears, N. 2001. "Time Pressure and Information in Sales Promotion Strategy: Conceptual Framework and Content Analysis." *Journal of Advertising* 30, no. 1, pp. 67–76.

Srinivasan, S.S., and R.E. Anderson. 1998. "Concepts and Strategy Guidelines for Designing Value Enhancing Sales Promotions." *Journal of Product & Brand Management* 7, no. 5, p. 410.

Srinivasan, S., K. Pauwels, D.M. Hanssens, and M.G. Dekimpe. 2004. "Do Promotions Benefit Manufacturers, Retailers, or Both?" *Management Science* 50, no. 5, pp. 617–29.

Stanley, J. 2003. "The Winner Is ...." *Marketing Management* 12, no. 1, pp. 46–48.

Stewart, D., and B. Gallen. 1998. "The Promotional Planning Process and Its Impact on Consumer Franchise Building: The Case of Fast-Moving Goods Companies in New Zealand." *Journal of Product & Brand Management* 7, no. 6, pp. 557–67.

Struse, R.W, III. 1987. "Approaches to Promotion Evaluation: A Practitioner's Viewpoint: Commentary." *Marketing Science* 6, no. 2, pp. 150–1.

Sun, B., S.A. Neslin, and K. Srinivasan. 2003. "Measuring the Impact of Promotions on Brand Switching When Consumers Are Forward Looking." *Journal of Marketing Research* 40, no. 4, pp. 389–405.

Townsend, M. 2011. "Discounts Could Make Christmas Not So Merry." *Bloomberg Businessweek* no. 4259, pp. 25–26.

Tseng, C.-H., Y.-C. Lou, and L.-T. Bei. 2009. "A Research of the Effect of Gift Promotion and Its Spillover Effect." *Advances in Consumer Research* 36, pp. 947–50.

Tsiros, M., and D.M. Hardesty. 2010. "Ending a Price Promotion: Retracting It in One Step or Phasing It Out Gradually." *Journal of Marketing* 74, no. 1, pp. 49–64.

van Heerde, H.J. 2005. "The Proper Interpretation of Sales Promotion Effects: Supplement Elasticities with Absolute Sales Effects." *Applied Stochastic Models in Business & Industry* 21, no. 4–5, pp. 397–402.

Vaughn, R. 1986. "How Advertising Works: a Planning Model Revisited." *Journal of Advertising Research* 26, no. 1, pp. 57–66.

Venkatesan, R., and P.W. Farris. 2012. "Measuring and Managing Returns from Retailer-Customized Coupon Campaigns." *Journal of Marketing* 76, no. 1, pp. 76–94. doi: 10.1509/jm.10.0162

Verhoef, P.C., and P.S.H. Leeflang. 2009. "Understanding the Marketing Department's Influence Within the Firm." *Journal of Marketing* 73, no. 2, pp. 14–37.

Volpe, R.J., and C. Li. 2012. "On the Frequency, Depth, and Duration of Sales at High-Low Pricing Supermarkets." *Agribusiness* 28, no. 2.

Wadhwa, M., B. Shiv, and S. Nowlis. 2006. "A Bite to Whet the Reward Appetite: Influence of Sampling on Appetitive Behaviors." *Advances in Consumer Research* 33, no. 1, p. 154.

Weber, J.H. 1963. "Can Results of Sales Promotion Be Predicted?" *Journal of Marketing* 27, no. 1, p. 15.

Webster, F.E., Jr. 2005. "A Perspective on the Evolution of Marketing Management." *Journal of Public Policy & Marketing* 24, no. 1, pp. 121–6.

Wei, W. 2007. "A Research Note: Evaluating Coupon Promotion Performance using Grey Target Theory." *Journal of Management Science* 1, no. 2, pp. 98–106.

Weiss, L., and R. Kivetz. 2011. When Not Redeeming a Coupon Feels Like Missing More Than Its Value. *Advances in Consumer Research-European Conference Proceedings*, 9, p. 517.

Wierenga, B., and H. Soethoudt. 2010. "Sales Promotions and Channel Coordination." *Journal of the Academy of Marketing Science* 38, no. 3, pp. 383–97.

Yadav, M.S., and K.B. Monroe. 1993. "How Buyers Perceive Savings in a Bundle Price: An Examination of a Bundle's Transaction Value." *Journal of Marketing Research* 30, no. 3, pp. 350–8.

Yi, Y., and J. Yoo. 2011. "The Long-Term Effects of Sales Promotions on Brand Attitude Across Monetary and Non-Monetary Promotions." *Psychology and Marketing* 28, no. 9, pp. 879–96.

Yin, R.K. 2003. *Case Study Research: Design and Methods*. 3rd ed. Thousand Oaks, CA: Sage Publications.

Zhang, Z.J., A. Krishna, and S.K. Dhar. 2000. "The Optimal Choice of Promotional Vehicles: Front-Loaded or Rear-Loaded Incentives?" *Management Science* 46, no. 3, pp. 348–62.

Ziliani, C. 2006. "Target Promotions: How to Measure and Improve Promotional Effectiveness Through Individual Customer Information." *Journal of Targeting, Measurement & Analysis for Marketing* 14, no. 3, pp. 249–59.

Index

OTHER TITLES IN OUR MARKETING STRATEGY COLLECTION

Naresh Malhotra, Georgia Tech, Editor

- *Developing Winning Brand Strategies* by Lars Finskud
- *Conscious Branding* by David Funk and Anne Marie Levis
- *Marketing Strategy in Play: Questioning to Create Difference* by Mark Hill
- *Decision Equity: The Ultimate Metric to Connect Marketing Actions to Profits* by Piyush Kumar and Kunal Gupta
- *Building a Marketing Plan: A Complete Guide* by Ho Yin Wong, Kylie Radel, and Roshnee Ramsaran-Fowdar
- *Top Market Strategy: Applying the 80/20 Rule* by Elizabeth Kruger
- *Pricing Segmentation and Analytics* by Tudor Bodea and Mark Ferguson
- *Strategic Marketing Planning for the Small to Medium Sized Business: Writing a Marketing Plan* by David Anderson
- *Expanding Customer Service as a Profit Center: Striving for Excellence and Competitive Advantage* by Rob Reider
- *Applying Scientific Reasoning to the Field of Marketing: Make Better Decisions* by Terry Grapentine
- *Marketing Strategy for Small- to Medium-Sized Manufacturers: A Practical Guide for Generating Growth, Profit, and Sales* by Charles E. France
- *Dynamic Customer Strategy: Today's CRM* by Jeff Tanner, Jr.
- *Customers Inside, Customers Outside: Designing and Succeeding With Enterprise Customer-Centricity Concepts, Practices, and Applications* by Michael W. Lowenstein
- *Developing Successful Marketing Strategies* by Gary W. Randazzo
- *Effective Advertising Strategies for Your Business* by Cong Li
- *Surprise!: The Secret to Customer Loyalty in the Service Sector* by Vincent P. Magnini

Announcing the Business Expert Press Digital Library

Concise e-books business students need for classroom and research

This book can also be purchased in an e-book collection by your library as

- a one-time purchase,
- that is owned forever,
- allows for simultaneous readers,
- has no restrictions on printing, and
- can be downloaded as PDFs from within the library community.

Our digital library collections are a great solution to beat the rising cost of textbooks. E-books can be loaded into their course management systems or onto students' e-book readers. The **Business Expert Press** digital libraries are very affordable, with no obligation to buy in future years. For more information, please visit **www.businessexpertpress.com/librarians**. To set up a trial in the United States, please email **sales@businessexpertpress.com**.

CPSIA information can be obtained
at www.ICGtesting.com
Printed in the USA
FFOW05n2037140115

9 781631 570476